센치한 Listening 길들이기

감성 맞춤 내신 공략

도약 **1**

센치한 LISTENING 길들이기 도약 1

지은이 | 신현겸, Brantley Smith
펴낸이 | 최회영
책임편집 | 김소연, 이수미
영문교열 | 이윤선, 윤은지, 강소영, Peggy Anderson
디자인 | 성윤지, 노영남, 이보람
펴낸곳 | (주)웅진컴퍼스
출판신고 | 1980년 3월 29일 제 406-2007-00046 © ㈜ 웅진씽크빅 2011
주소 | 서울특별시 서초구 강남대로 39길 15-10 한라비발디스튜디오 193 3층
전화 | (02)3471- 0096
홈페이지 | http://www.compasspub.com
ISBN | 978-89-6697-779-6

10 9 8 7 6 5 4 3
20 19 18 17 16

01

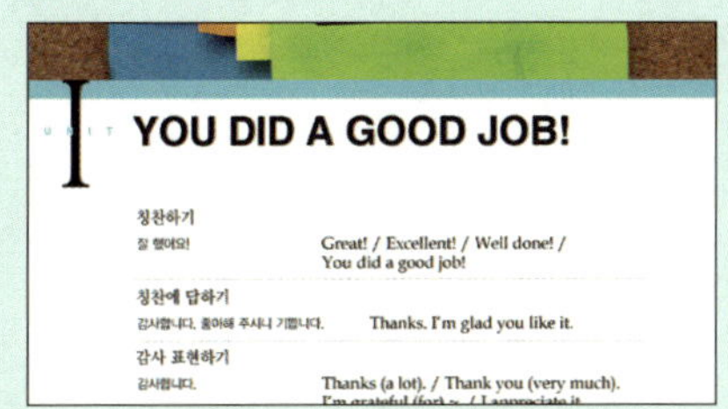

Introduction

Unit에서 학습의 초점이 되는 주요 의사소통 기능과 예문들을 먼저 학습합니다.

02

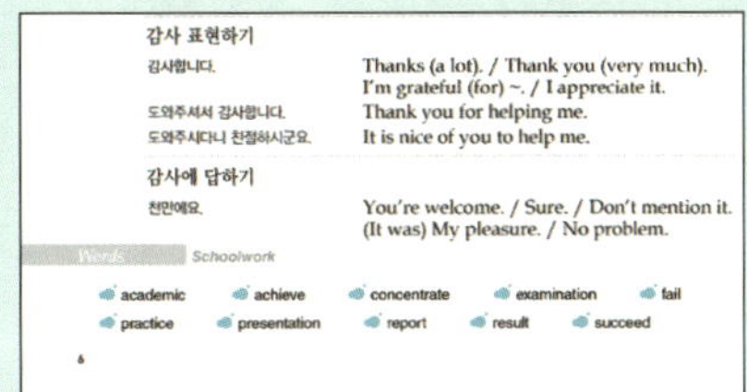

Words

듣기평가에서 자주 출제되는 특정 주제의 중요 어휘를 익힙니다.

03

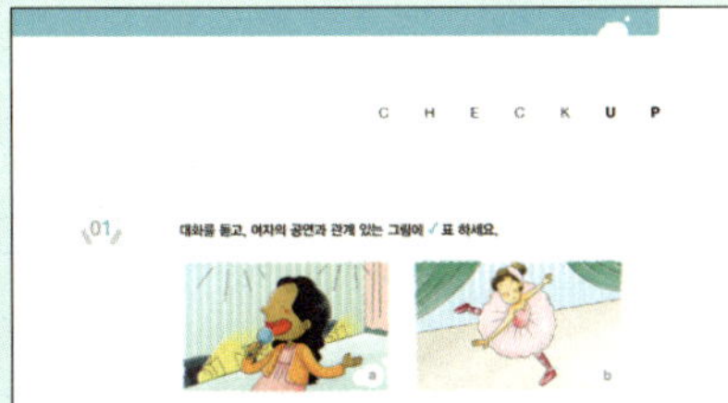

Check Up

01–02. 앞서 배운 의사소통 기능을 중심으로 구성된 짧은 내용을 듣고, 간단한 연습 문제를 풀어봅니다.
03. 빈칸에 알맞은 의사소통 표현을 써 보면서 해당 표현들을 확실히 기억합니다.

04

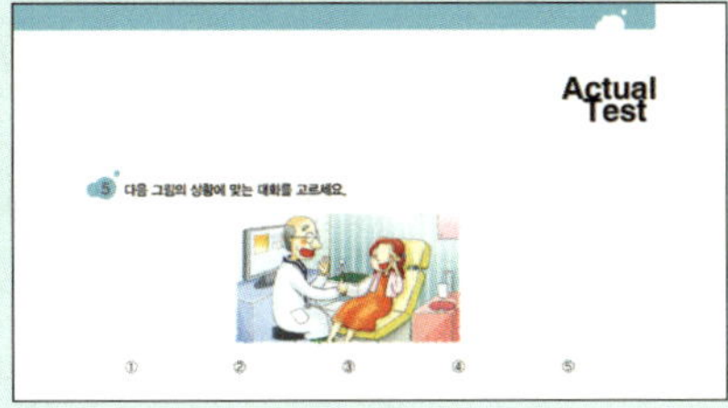

Actual Test

핵심 의사소통 기능을 포함한 내용으로 구성된 8문항의 문제를 풀어봅니다.
다양한 유형의 실전 듣기평가 문제 유형을 익힐 수 있습니다.

05

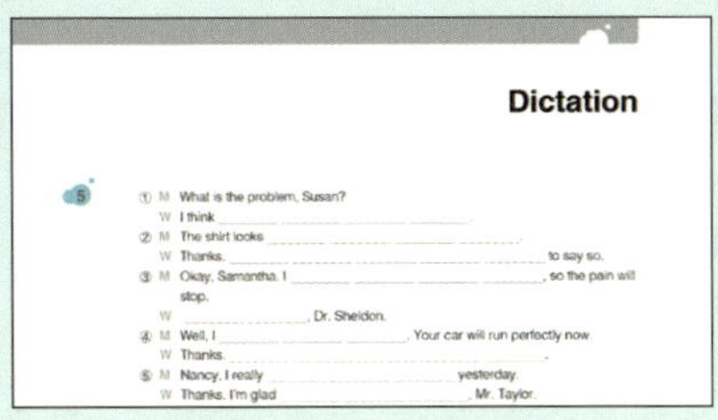

Dictation

Actual Test 8문항의 스크립트를 다시 듣고 빈칸을 채우면서 주요 표현과 어휘를 복습합니다.

06

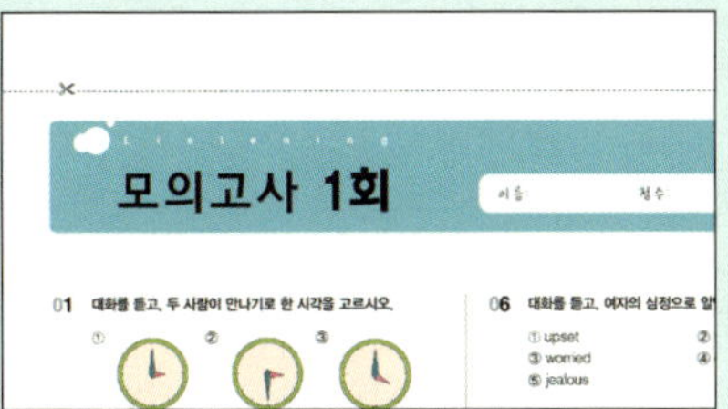

모의고사

실전과 똑같은 스타일로 구성된 총 3회의 모의고사를 통해 실제 듣기평가 시험에 완벽 대비합니다.

Table of Contents

A Separate-Volume Supplement : Answers and Audio scripts . MP3 File CD

I YOU DID A GOOD JOB!

칭찬하기

잘 했어요!

Great! / Excellent! / Well done! /
You did a good job!

칭찬에 답하기

감사합니다. 좋아해 주시니 기뻐요.　Thanks. I'm glad you like it.

감사 표현하기

감사합니다.

Thanks (a lot). / Thank you (very much).
I'm grateful (for) ~. / I appreciate it.

도와주셔서 감사합니다.　Thank you for helping me.

도와주시다니 친절하시군요.　It is nice of you to help me.

감사에 답하기

천만에요.

You're welcome. / Sure. / Don't mention it.
My pleasure. / No problem.

Words　*Schoolwork*

 academic　 achieve　 concentrate　 examination　fail

 practice　 presentation　 report　 result　succeed

대화를 듣고, 여자의 공연과 관계 있는 그림에 ✓ 표 하세요.

대화를 듣고, 내용과 일치하도록 괄호 안에서 알맞은 말을 고르세요.

1 The man (sold, fixed) the woman's watch.
2 The woman will give the man (15 dollars, 50 dollars).

03

주어진 표현을 사용하여 대화를 완성하세요.

My pleasure	I'm really grateful
don't mention it	Thank you for helping me

A ____________________ find my dog yesterday. I was really worried about him.

B ____________________. Is he doing OK now?

A Yeah, he wasn't hurt or scared. Again, ____________________ for your help.

B Oh, ____________________.

들려주는 내용을 잘 듣고 물음에 답하세요.

1 대화를 듣고, 여자의 자동차 키가 발견된 곳을 고르세요.

2 대화를 듣고, 남자가 여자에게 전화를 한 이유를 고르세요.

① 결혼을 축하하기 위해 ② 결혼식에 초대하기 위해 ③ 결혼식 날짜를 묻기 위해
④ 약속을 취소하기 위해 ⑤ 약속을 변경하기 위해

3 대화를 듣고, 두 사람의 관계로 알맞은 것을 고르세요.

① 어머니 – 아들 ② 교사 – 학부모 ③ 교사 – 학생
④ 사장 – 비서 ⑤ 사장 – 사원

4 대화를 듣고, 대화가 일어나고 있는 장소를 고르세요.

① at a mall ② at a movie theater ③ at a bookstore
④ at a library ⑤ at a post office

5 다음 그림의 상황에 맞는 대화를 고르세요.

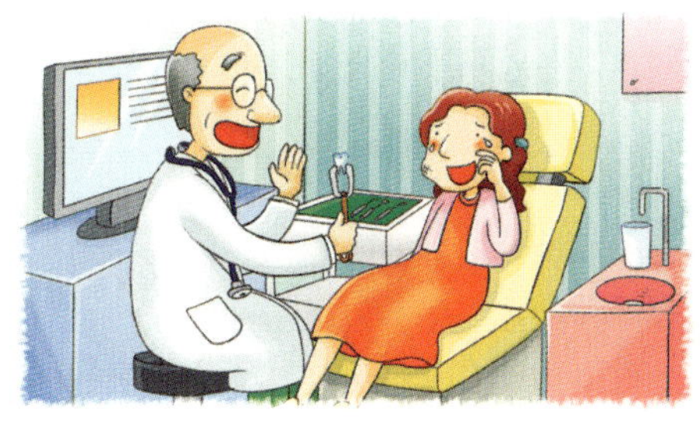

①   ②   ③   ④   ⑤

6 대화를 듣고, 여자의 심정으로 알맞은 것을 고르세요.

① sad   ② angry   ③ nervous
④ proud   ⑤ calm

7 대화를 듣고, 남자의 말에 이어질 여자의 응답으로 알맞은 것을 고르세요.

W ______________________________

① You did a good job.
② Thanks, I'm glad you like it.
③ Let's go out for dinner.
④ We should be thankful for the food.
⑤ Don't use so much pepper next time.

8 다음을 듣고, 언급되지 <u>않은</u> 것을 고르세요.

① 행사가 열린 장소   ② 행사가 열린 시기   ③ 행사를 열게 된 목적
④ 행사의 총 수익금   ⑤ 행사에서 가장 많이 팔린 음식

다음을 듣고 빈칸에 들어갈 알맞은 말을 쓰세요.

1

M Hey, Deborah. __________ __________ __________?

W Yeah. I can't find __________ __________ __________ anywhere.

M Oh no! Where did you have them last?

W I put them __________ __________ __________ __________, but they fell out somewhere. I thought they fell out on the couch, but __________ __________ __________ __________, either.

M Oh, here! They were lying __________ __________ __________.

W Thank you for __________ __________ __________ __________.

2

W Hello?

M Hi, Annette. It's Phillip.

W Oh, Phillip! It's been a while. __________ __________ __________ __________?

M I'm doing OK. I heard that __________ __________ __________ recently.

W Yeah, I got married to Arnold last month.

M Excellent! I'm happy __________ __________ __________. I wish you both the best.

W __________ __________ __________.

3

W Tim, I'd like to speak with you.

M Sure, Mrs. Jenner. __________ __________ __________ __________?

W Oh, not at all. I thought you did well on your presentation the other day.

M Thanks for saying that. __________ __________ __________ __________ on it.

W I know. The other students should __________ __________ __________. Again, __________ __________.

M My pleasure.

4

M Excuse me. I'd like to __________ __________ __________ __________ by Stephen King. Do you have __________ __________ __________ __________?

W Yes, sir. It's in the fiction section.

M __________ __________ __________?

W It's at the front, __________ __________ __________ __________ and magazine sections.

M Thank you so much.

W Oh, __________ __________ __________.

5

① M What is the problem, Susan?

　 W I think _________ _________ _________ _________.

② M The shirt looks _________ _________ _________ _________.

　 W Thanks. _________ _________ _________ _________ _________ to say so.

③ M Okay, Samantha. I _________ _________ _________ _________, so the pain will

　　 stop.

　 W _________ _________, Dr. Sheldon.

④ M Well, I _________ _________ _________. Your car will run perfectly now.

　 W Thanks. _________ _________ _________ _________ _________.

⑤ M Nancy, I really _________ _________ _________ yesterday.

　 W Thanks. I'm glad _________ _________ _________, Mr. Taylor.

6

M Guess what, Mom? I _________ _________ _________ for my science project

　 today!

W That's great! What was _________ _________ _________ again?

M I made a model of _________ _________ _________. The teacher said it was

　 _________ _________ _________ she'd ever seen. She even said I should

　 _________ _________.

W Wonderful! _________ _________ _________ _________ _________.

7

W Are you _________ _________ _________, Sam?

M Yeah, it's delicious. I didn't know you could _________ _________ _________,

　 Tammy.

W Well, I just used _________ _________ _________ _________. I added

　 _________ _________ _________, though.

M That must be _________ _________ _________ _________. Still, I think it's

　 _________ _________ _________.

8

W Good morning, class. Today I have the results of _________ _________ _________

　 this past weekend. We raised _________ _________ _________ for the poor African

　 children! _________ _________, everybody. Tammy's fudge brownies sold more

　 than _________ _________ _________. Those brownies alone made over 500

　 dollars! Great job. All in all, it was _________ _________ _________.

UNIT II — WILL YOU DO ME A FAVOR?

도움 요청하기

~을 해 주실 수 있나요?	Can/Could you ~, please?
제 부탁을 들어주실 수 있나요?	Can/Would/Will you do me a favor?
	Can I ask you a favor?
제가 ~하는 것을 도와주시겠어요?	Would you please help me ~?

도움 요청에 답하기

물론이죠. 무슨 일인가요?	Sure (I can). / Of course. What is it?
죄송하지만 (~때문에) 도와드릴 수 없어요.	I'm afraid I can't (because) ~.

Words　　*Repair Shop*

- broken
- condition
- damage
- engine
- engineer
- expert
- fix
- machine
- necessary
- repair
- request

대화를 듣고, Ann이 부탁받은 일에 ✓ 표 하세요.

대화를 듣고, 내용과 일치하면 T, 일치하지 않으면 F에 ✓ 표 하세요.

1 Jane left her wallet at home.　　　　　　T　F
2 Robert will lend Jane 10 dollars.　　　　T　F

03 주어진 표현을 사용하여 대화를 완성하세요.

Can I use your computer	What is it
Sure, you can	can I ask you a favor

A Andrew, ___________________________?

B Of course. ___________________________?

A I have to type a paper for history class tomorrow, but my computer just broke down. ___________________________?

B ___________________________.

들려주는 내용을 잘 듣고 물음에 답하세요.

1 대화를 듣고, 은행의 위치를 고르세요.

2 대화를 듣고, 남자의 심정으로 알맞은 것을 고르세요.

① worried　　② hopeful　　③ thankful
④ relaxed　　⑤ lonely

3 다음을 듣고, 남자가 여자에게 부탁한 일이 <u>아닌</u> 것을 고르세요.

4 대화를 듣고, 이어질 여자의 행동으로 알맞은 것을 고르세요.

① 수리공을 부른다.　　　② Bob에게 전화를 한다.
③ 새 TV를 사러 간다.　　④ Marvin의 집을 방문한다.
⑤ DVD 플레이어를 빌린다.

5 다음 그림의 상황에 맞는 대화를 고르세요.

①   ②   ③   ④   ⑤

6 다음을 듣고, 무엇에 관한 내용인지 고르세요.

① 전기의 역할   ② 지진의 원인
③ 지진의 피해   ④ 수질 오염의 심각성
⑤ 수질 오염 해결 방안

7 대화를 듣고, 여자가 남자에게 부탁한 일을 고르세요.

① To give her a ride   ② To drive her car
③ To repair her car   ④ To go to a repair shop
⑤ To teach her how to drive

8 대화를 듣고, 내용과 일치하지 <u>않는</u> 것을 고르세요.

① 여자는 남자에게 파티 준비를 부탁하고 있다.
② Cindy를 위한 파티는 금요일에 열린다.
③ Cindy는 새 학교 때문에 이사할 예정이다.
④ 남자의 할머니는 입원 중이다.
⑤ 여자는 수요일에 케이크를 준비할 것이다.

다음을 듣고 빈칸에 들어갈 알맞은 말을 쓰세요.

1

M Excuse me, ma'am? _________ _________ _________ _________?

W _________ _________. What is it?

M I'm _________ _________ _________ _________, but I don't know this area very well. _________ _________ _________ where it is?

W Yeah. _________ _________ on Jackson Street until you reach the coffee shop. Then _________ _________. The bank is _________ _________ _________ on your right.

M Thanks.

2

M Annette, I _________ _________ _________ _________ for my math test, but I'm not _________ _________ _________. Can you help me?

W Sorry, I'm afraid I can't. I'm meeting my friends _________ _________ _________ tonight.

M Aw, but that test is tomorrow!

W Well, I'm sorry, but _________ _________ _________ _________ tonight.

M Oh, _________ _________ _________ _________ then? My mom will be very upset if _________ _________ _________ _________ again.

3

M Hey, Linda, it's John. Will you _________ _________ _________ _________? My family and I _________ _________ _________ next week. Could you get our mail and _________ _________ _________ while we're away? And you know that _________ _________ _________ _________. Since we can't take him, I hope you can _________ _________ _________ _________ every day. If you can do it, call me back. Talk to you later!

4

W Marvin, _________ _________ _________ _________ with something?

M What do you need?

W Well, my television _________ _________ _________. Could you look at it?

M I can only _________ _________ _________. But my friend Bob knows a lot about TVs. Why don't you _________ _________ _________ _________? Here's his phone number.

W Thanks!

5

① W I can't ______ ______ ______ here.
  M Oh, I ______ ______ ______ in my room.
② W Oh, these boxes are ______ ______. Will you please help me?
  M Sure. ______ ______ ______ ______ to me.
③ W Do you know ______ ______ ______ ______?
  M I have no idea. Why don't you ______ ______ ______ ______?
④ W Hey, ______ ______ ______? You look tired.
  M I had ______ ______ ______ ______ at school today.
⑤ W It's ______ ______ ______. I think we should just stay home.
  M ______ ______ ______ ______.

6

W It has been almost three months, but half of our city ______ ______ ______ ______. Many people lost their homes and lives ______ ______ ______ ______. And many people need help now. Millions in the city are still without ______ ______ ______. It is said that it will take many years to repair ______ ______ ______.

7

W Hey, Jack, can you ______ ______ ______ ______?
M Sure. What is it?
W My car is ______ ______ ______ ______, and I need a ride to the Park Office Building after work. ______ ______ ______ ______?
M Sure. I'll go to your office by 7 p.m. ______ ______ ______?
W Yeah, ______ ______ ______.

8

W Could you do me a favor, Robbie?
M Of course. ______ ______ ______ ______?
W I need help preparing a special cake for Cindy's party. ______ ______ ______ for her new school, so we're having a party for her on Friday.
M ______ ______ ______ ______ the cake?
W The day before the party.
M Oh, sorry, I have to ______ ______ ______ on that day.
W Oh, I heard that your grandmother is ______ ______ ______ now. I hope ______ ______ ______ ______.
M Thanks.

<h1>U N I T III — ARE YOU SURE?</h1>

확신 여부 묻기

~을 확신하나요?	Are you sure ~?
~라고 생각하나요?	Do you think (that) ~?

확신, 불확신 표현하기

저는 ~라고 확신합니다.	I'm sure (that) ~.
저는 그것에 대해 확신합니다.	I'm pretty sure about that.
~에 대해 확신하지는 않습니다.	I'm not sure about ~.
그는 아마 ~할지도 모릅니다.	He will probably ~.

Words   **Daily Life**

- appointment
- attend
- be busy -ing
- enjoy -ing
- exercise
- invitation
- park
- repeat
- schedule
- spend
- take care of
- take part in

01 대화를 듣고, Chris의 심정을 나타낸 그림을 골라 ✓ 표 하세요.

02 대화를 듣고, 내용과 일치하도록 보기에서 알맞은 말을 골라 써넣으세요.

fix his car	wash his father's car	play baseball	play basketball

→ Bill will ___________________ and ___________________ with his friends
  on Saturday afternoon.

03 주어진 표현을 사용하여 대화를 완성하세요.

I'm pretty sure	Are you sure	Do you think we'll be seated soon

A We've been waiting for nearly 20 minutes.
  ___________________________?
B Don't worry. We'll be seated soon.
A ___________________________?
B Yeah, ___________________________ it will be just a few more minutes.
A I hope so. I'm really hungry.

들려주는 내용을 잘 듣고 물음에 답하세요.

1 대화를 듣고, 여자의 직업으로 알맞은 것을 고르세요.

①   ②   ③   ④   ⑤

2 대화를 듣고, Kevin의 생일이 언제인지 고르세요.

① 6월 15일   ② 6월 21일   ③ 6월 22일   ④ 6월 29일   ⑤ 6월 30일

3 대화를 듣고, 두 사람의 관계로 알맞은 것을 고르세요.

① 사장 – 비서   ② 승무원 – 승객
③ 음식점 점원 – 지배인   ④ 면접관 – 구직자
⑤ 음식점 점원 – 손님

4 대화를 듣고, 이어서 들려주는 질문에 알맞은 답을 고르세요.

① Boston   ② Chicago
③ Buffalo   ④ New York
⑤ Washington D.C.

5 다음을 듣고, 여자가 무엇에 관해 이야기하고 있는지 고르세요.

① a piano   ② a violin
③ the drums   ④ a guitar
⑤ a flute

6 대화를 듣고, 아래 일정표에서 <u>잘못된</u> 것을 고르세요.

	Friday	Saturday	Sunday
Louis	① 12 p.m. to 8 p.m.	12 p.m. to 8 p.m.	OFF
Ryan	② 12 p.m. to 8 p.m.	2 p.m. to 8 p.m.	③ OFF
Nick	12 p.m. to 4 p.m.	④ OFF	⑤ 2 p.m. to 6 p.m.

7 대화를 듣고, 남자의 말에 이어질 여자의 응답으로 알맞은 것을 고르세요.

W

① I hope you'll get better soon.
② I think your project was excellent.
③ Sorry, but I don't think I can do it.
④ Why don't you ask Liz for help? She is free.
⑤ Are you sure? Let me know if you need more time.

8 대화를 듣고, 남자가 주장하는 바를 고르세요.

① 학생의 수를 줄여야 한다.
② 학교 시설을 확장해야 한다.
③ 학교 규칙을 강화해야 한다.
④ 학교의 예산을 삭감해야 한다.
⑤ 자율적인 학습 분위기를 조성해야 한다.

다음을 듣고 빈칸에 들어갈 알맞은 말을 쓰세요.

1

M ____________ ____________ ____________ __________, ma'am?

W Sure. What is it?

M Someone __________ ____________ __________ from school.

W I see. __________ __________ __________ it was stolen?

M Yes, I'm sure. __________ __________ __________ in the same place. Do you think you will __________ __________ __________?

W I'm not sure about that, but __________ __________ __________.

2

M Hey, today is Kevin's birthday, right?

W No. His birthday is __________ __________ __________ __________.

M __________ __________ __________? I thought his birthday is __________ __________.

W I'm sure. __________ __________ __________ yesterday.

3

W __________ __________ __________ __________, sir?

M Yes, everything was wonderful. I especially __________ __________ __________.

W Excellent. Are you sure that you wouldn't like some dessert? We __________ __________ __________ __________.

M Yes, I'm sure. __________ __________. I appreciate it, though.

W __________ __________ __________ __________, then.

M Thank you.

4

M Hey, Janice, __________ __________ __________ __________?

W It was nice. I drove up to Boston __________ __________ __________ __________.

M __________ __________ __________?

W Okay. She said that my sister just __________ __________ __________ __________ in New York. She'll move to New York next month.

M Great! She __________ __________ __________.

W Yeah, but she's also sad because she __________ __________ __________ __________ Buffalo. She __________ __________ __________ __________ there.

M I see. __________ __________ __________ she will love the city.

5

W Playing this instrument ___________ ___________ ___________. I love ___________ ___________ ___________ by Mozart. I also love ___________ ___________ for my friends. The ___________ ___________ ___________ ___________ exercise my fingers and my mind. I'm sure I will become ___________ ___________ ___________ one day.

6

M Hey, have you made out the schedule for this weekend, yet?

W Yeah. Louis and Ryan are both ___________ ___________ ___________ ___________ on Friday: from 12 p.m. to 8 p.m.

M Great. ___________ ___________ ___________?

W Louis, Ryan, and Nick ___________ ___________ ___________ that day. ___________ ___________ ___________ that's enough people?

M I'm sure ___________ ___________ ___________ ___________.

W Oh, and Nick is coming in ___________ ___________ ___________ ___________ ___________: from 2 p.m. to 6 p.m. He'll be ___________ ___________.

M That's fine.

7

W Jason, ___________ ___________ ___________ from Liz?

M Yes, Ms. Dalton. I know ___________ ___________ ___________.

W So your partner for your class project ___________ ___________ ___________. Do you think that ___________ ___________ ___________ ___________?

M Yeah, ___________ ___________ ___________. We're almost done. I can finish ___________ ___________ ___________ ___________ by myself.

8

W Well, ___________ ___________ ___________ ___________ begins in a few days.

M I know. There are going to be ___________ ___________ ___________ ___________ ___________ in my grade this year.

W Whoa! That's a lot.

M I know. I think we should ___________ ___________ ___________ for these new students.

W Are you sure ___________ ___________ ___________ ___________? That would cost ___________ ___________ ___________ ___________.

M Well, we have to do something. There are ___________ ___________ ___________ in our school.

IV TAKE IT EASY!

감정 묻고 답하기

기분이 어떤가요?	How do you feel? / How are you feeling?
왜 그렇게 기분이 나빠요?	Why are you so angry/upset/mad?
기분이 아주 좋아요.	I feel great/wonderful/fantastic.
전 굉장히 화가 났어요.	I'm really angry/upset/mad.

감정 가라앉히기

진정하렴.	Relax. / Take it easy. / Calm down.

동정 표현하기

안됐군요.	That's too bad. / It's a pity. What a pity! / I'm sorry to hear that.

Words *Feelings*

- awful
- confused
- disappointed
- gloomy
- hopeful
- pleased
- proud
- relaxed
- scared
- terrible

01 대화를 듣고, 상황에 알맞은 그림에 ✓ 표 하세요.

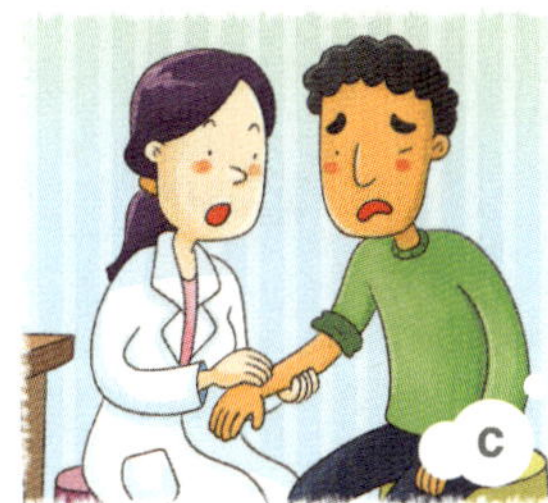

02 대화를 듣고, Kevin이 Ms. Sharp를 찾아온 이유를 골라 ✓ 표 하세요.

a 성적을 확인하기 위해 ☐

b 수학문제의 풀이 방법을 묻기 위해 ☐

c 교우 관계로 인한 고민을 상담하기 위해 ☐

03 주어진 표현을 사용하여 대화를 완성하세요.

I'm really upset	calm down
How are you	Why are you so upset

A Good morning, Linda. _______________________?

B _______________________.

A _______________________?

B Because my brother broke my glasses.

A Hey, _______________________.

들려주는 내용을 잘 듣고 물음에 답하세요.

1 대화를 듣고, 여자의 가방 속에 있던 물건이 <u>아닌</u> 것을 고르세요.

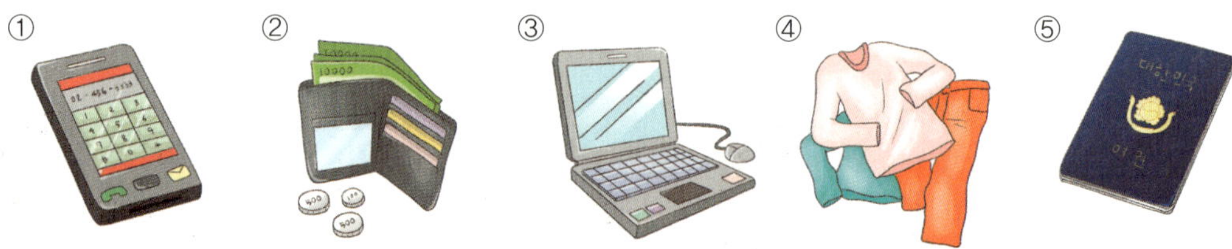

① ② ③ ④ ⑤

2 대화를 듣고, Jeremy의 여동생에 관한 사실로 언급된 것을 고르세요.

① 운전을 잘 하지 못한다.
② 지난 주말에 교통 사고를 당했다.
③ 현재 다리가 불편한 상태이다.
④ 어릴 때부터 몸이 허약했다.
⑤ 최근 병원에서 퇴원을 했다.

3 대화를 듣고, 메모한 내용 중 <u>잘못된</u> 것을 고르세요.

① To: Dr. Smith
② From: Melissa Hart
③ Reason: Needs heart medicine
④ Appointment for Tuesday, 10 a.m.
⑤ Call back at 555-6799

4 대화를 듣고, 남자의 나이를 고르세요.

① 20살　　② 25살　　③ 30살　　④ 33살　　⑤ 35살

5 다음을 듣고, 남자가 전화를 건 목적을 고르세요.

① 승진 축하   ② 취업 문의   ③ 해고 통보
④ 면접 결과 통보   ⑤ 일자리 제안

6 다음 중 어색한 대화를 고르세요.

①   ②   ③   ④   ⑤

7 다음을 듣고, 호텔의 장점으로 언급되지 <u>않은</u> 것을 고르세요.

① 지리적 위치가 편리하다.   ② 서비스가 훌륭하다.
③ 넓은 객실을 구비하고 있다.   ④ 아름다운 경관을 즐길 수 있다.
⑤ 고급 레스토랑의 음식을 즐길 수 있다.

8 대화를 듣고, 남자의 말에 이어질 여자의 응답으로 알맞은 것을 고르세요.

W ____________________________________

① I'm looking forward to it.
② Be careful when you drive.
③ Calm down. I think you need to take a break.
④ I don't have any work to do now.
⑤ Don't worry. You'll do better next time.

1

W Excuse me! ___________ ___________ ___________ ___________ ___________?

M Yes, ma'am. ___________ ___________ ___________?

W I think ___________ ___________ ___________ ___________! We just landed and it's not here! ___________ ___________ ___________ was in there!

M All right, ___________ ___________ ___________.

W But that suitcase had everything in it! My laptop computer, ___________ ___________, and ___________ ___________.

M All right. I'll get someone ___________ ___________ ___________ right away.

2

W Jeremy, ___________ ___________ ___________. What's wrong?

M My sister ___________ ___________ ___________ ___________ last weekend. She ___________ ___________ ___________.

W Oh, I'm sorry ___________ ___________ ___________. Is she OK?

M Yeah, she's getting better, but I'm still ___________ ___________ ___________.

3

M ___________ ___________ ___________ today, Dr. Smith?

W ___________ ___________ ___________. It's been very busy, though.

M By the way, Melissa Hart called. She ___________ ___________ ___________ ___________ for Thursday at 10 a.m.

W I see. ___________ ___________ ___________ ___________?

M She says it's ___________ ___________ ___________. She needs more of it.

W Okay. Did she ___________ ___________ ___________?

M Yes. It's 555-6799.

W Okay. ___________ ___________ ___________ ___________.

4

M Hey, Tammy. How are you today?

W Well, I'm ___________ ___________ ___________, Mr. Potter. ___________ ___________ ___________ ___________ of this school.

M Ah, I know how that feels.

W Really?

M Yeah, I remember ___________ ___________ ___________ at this school 20 years ago. I was just a nervous 13-year-old kid entering ___________ ___________, ___________ ___________. But don't worry! You'll ___________ ___________ ___________ with everyone.

5 M Hello, Barry. This is Jim. I heard your brother's company ________ ________ ________. I'm sorry to hear that. I know that it is hard ________ ________ ________ now. In fact, I think that my uncle's company will have ________ ________ ________ ________ soon. If your brother is interested, please ________ ________ ________. Bye.

6
① M ________ ________ ________ ________ today?
　 W ________ ________ ________.
② M Are you feeling OK?
　 W Well, I hope ________ ________ ________.
③ M I didn't ________ ________ ________ ________.
　 W Oh, ________ ________ ________.
④ M Oh, I think ________ ________ ________ ________.
　 W ________ ________. It will be okay.
⑤ M My grandfather ________ ________ ________.
　 W I'm sorry ________ ________ ________.

---

7 W Are you ________ ________ ________ out of town? Then plan your stay at the Swan Hotel. You can ________ ________ ________ and enjoy beautiful views here. And our hotels are famous ________ ________ ________ ________ and greatest service around. We also have five-star restaurants, and you'll love ________ ________ ________. So what are you waiting for? ________ ________ ________ today!

---

8 W Ted, ________ ________ ________. What's wrong?
M Oh, ________ ________ ________. I hate my reading club!
W Why? I thought ________ ________ ________ ________.
M Not at all. There's just ________ ________ ________ to do. ________ ________ ________ ________!

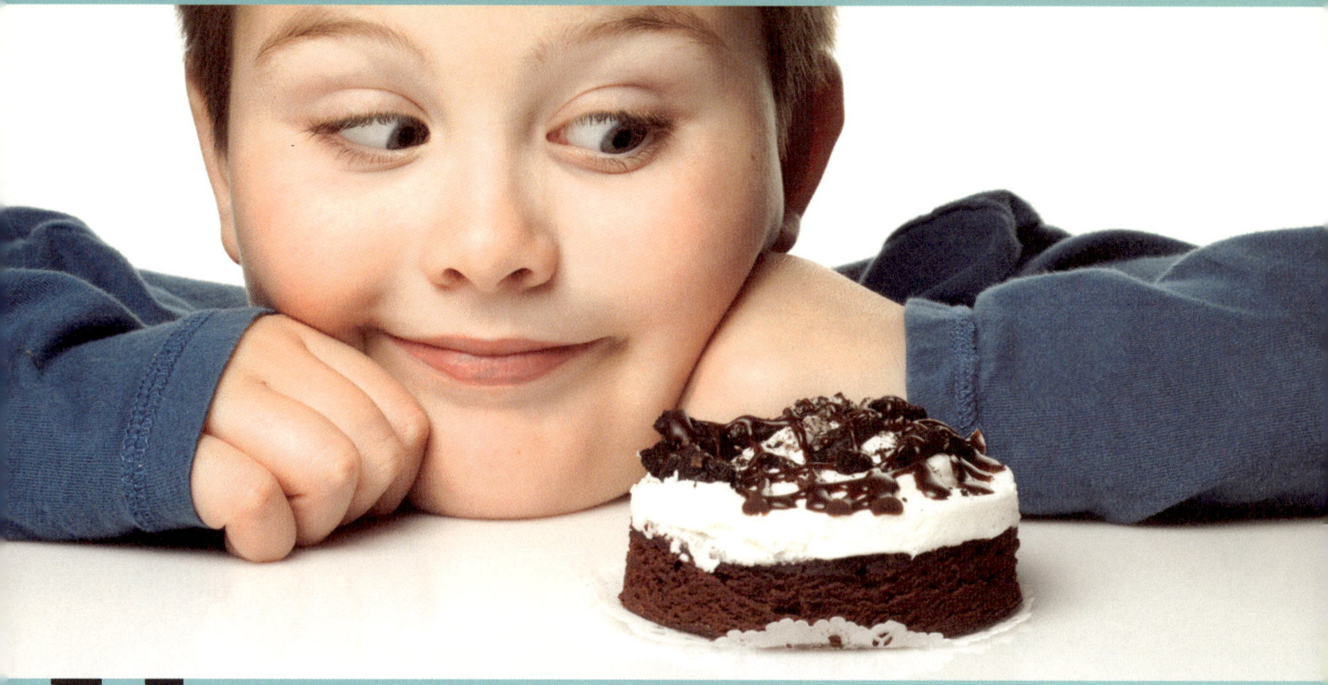

UNIT V

HELP YOURSELF.

음식 권유하기

~을 드시겠어요?	Would you like (some) ~?
~을 더 드시겠어요?	Do you want some more ~?
~을 마음껏 드세요.	Help yourself (to ~).

음식 권유에 답하기

감사합니다. 정말 맛있군요.	Thanks. I really love it.
네, 더 주세요.	Yes, please. / Yes, thank you.
감사하지만 괜찮습니다.	No, thanks.
감사하지만 배가 부르군요.	Thanks, but I'm full.

Words **Food**

- bake
- boil
- dairy
- flavor
- grill
- grocery
- junk food
- spicy
- sour
- tasty
- unhealthy

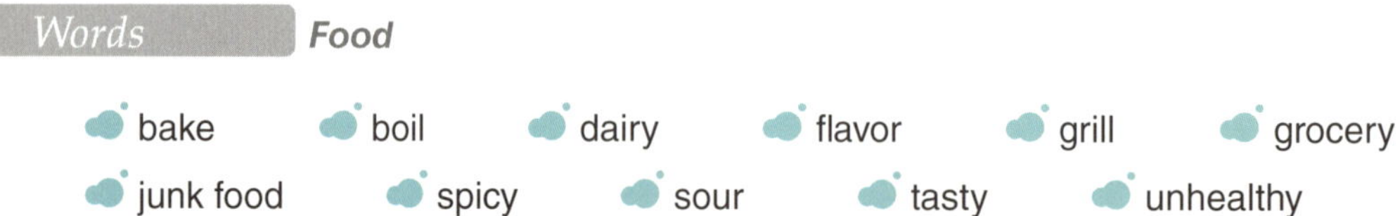

 대화를 듣고, 두 사람이 사게 될 과일을 모두 골라 ✓ 표 하세요.

a

b

c

d

 대화를 듣고, 대화가 일어나고 있는 장소를 고르세요.

a in a classroom

b in a cafeteria

c in an office

03 주어진 표현을 사용하여 대화를 완성하세요.

| Yes, please | I'm full |
| Do you want some more pizza | Would you like |

A _________________________?

B Thanks, but _____________________.

A _____________________ some more soda then?

B _____________________.

A Here you are.

들려주는 내용을 잘 듣고 물음에 답하세요.

1 다음을 듣고, 각 그림의 상황과 어울리지 <u>않는</u> 설명을 고르세요.

①  ②  ③  ④  ⑤ 

2 대화를 듣고, 여자가 걱정하는 이유를 고르세요.

① 아들이 비만이라서
② 아들의 편식이 심해서
③ 아들이 게을러서
④ 아들의 성격이 비관적이라서
⑤ 아들이 무리한 다이어트를 해서

3 다음을 듣고, 글의 목적으로 알맞은 것을 고르세요.

① 광고　　　　② 감사　　　　③ 사과　　　　④ 항의　　　　⑤ 문의

4 대화를 듣고, 여자의 취미가 무엇인지 고르세요.

① Drawing pictures
② Collecting toys
③ Making her own coffee
④ Taking photographs
⑤ Collecting coffee mugs

5 대화를 듣고, 남자가 주문한 음식을 알맞게 나타낸 그림을 고르세요.

①  ②  ③  ④  ⑤ 

6 대화를 듣고, 케이크의 원래 가격이 얼마인지 고르세요.

① $3 ② $5 ③ $6 ④ $9 ⑤ $12

7 대화를 듣고, 내용과 일치하는 것을 고르세요.

① The man doesn't like the color of the kitchen.
② The woman painted her kitchen.
③ The woman sold her old table.
④ The woman's new table was expensive.
⑤ The man bought a new table for the woman.

8 대화를 듣고, 남자의 말에 이어질 여자의 응답으로 알맞은 것을 고르세요.

W ______________________________

① It's Saturday afternoon.
② Thanks, but I'm full.
③ Sure, I really love to cook.
④ We'll meet at Jennifer's house.
⑤ We'll have hot dogs, hamburgers, and steaks.

다음을 듣고 빈칸에 들어갈 알맞은 말을 쓰세요.

1

W ① He ___________ ___________ ___________.

② She ___________ ___________ ___________ ___________.

③ He is buying ___________ ___________.

④ They ___________ ___________ ___________.

⑤ She ___________ ___________ ___________ with the knife.

2

W Come on, Timmy. You haven't eaten ___________ ___________.

M No, ___________ ___________. ___________ ___________, Mom.

W But ___________ ___________ ___________ ___________ ___________. You need to eat some.

M Oh, Mom. You know ___________ ___________ ___________ ___________. I don't like

___________ ___________ ___________ ___________.

W Oh, Timmy. ___________ ___________ ___________ about you.

3

M Do you want ___________ ___________ ___________? Then try East Seas Ramen Noodles! There are over ___________ ___________ ___________ of noodles. ___________ ___________ ___________ ___________ a bag of potato chips or crackers, too. All you have to do is ___________ ___________, ___________, and enjoy! You can ___________ ___________ ___________ in any grocery or convenience store, too. So ___________ ___________ ___________ East Seas Ramen Noodles today!

4

W This is excellent coffee. Can I ___________ ___________ ___________, please?

M ___________. Help yourself.

W Also, do you sell ___________ ___________ ___________ like this? I'd like to add it ___________ ___________ ___________.

M You have ___________ ___________ ___________ ___________. I think we have ___________ ___________ ___________ ___________ in the gift shop.

W Oh, I would like to see ___________ ___________ ___________ ___________.

M Sure. Come this way.

Dictation

5

W Good day, sir. _________ _________ _________ _________ _________ one of our fish plates?

M _________ _________ _________ _________, please. Can I have the fish _________ _________ _________, please?

W Sure. You can also order _________ _________ _________ with that dish.

M Hmm. _________ _________ _________ _________ with that, please.

W All right. Will there be _________ _________, sir?

M _________ _________ _________ _________, thank you.

6

W Would you like _________ _________?

M Yes, I'd like to have chocolate cake. It says here that _________ _________ _________ now. Is that right?

W Yes, sir. _________ _________ _________ _________ now.

M Oh, great. _________ _________ _________.

7

M It's so good to see you again, Aunt Ruth.

W It's good _________ _________ _________ _________, Ryan. Do you want _________ _________ _________?

M No, thanks, _________ _________. Say, did you paint your kitchen?

W Yes. We _________ _________ _________ a new color.

M It looks really nice.

W Thank you. _________ _________ _________ _________. I also got a _________ _________.

M I see that. Did you sell _________ _________ _________?

W No. It's in our bedroom.

8

W Would you like _________ _________ _________, Eddie?

M Yes, please. _________ _________ _________ _________, Wendy.

W Thanks. I think _________ _________ _________ to my neighborhood cookout then. I'll cook _________ _________ _________ _________ on the grill.

M That sounds great. _________ _________ _________ _________?

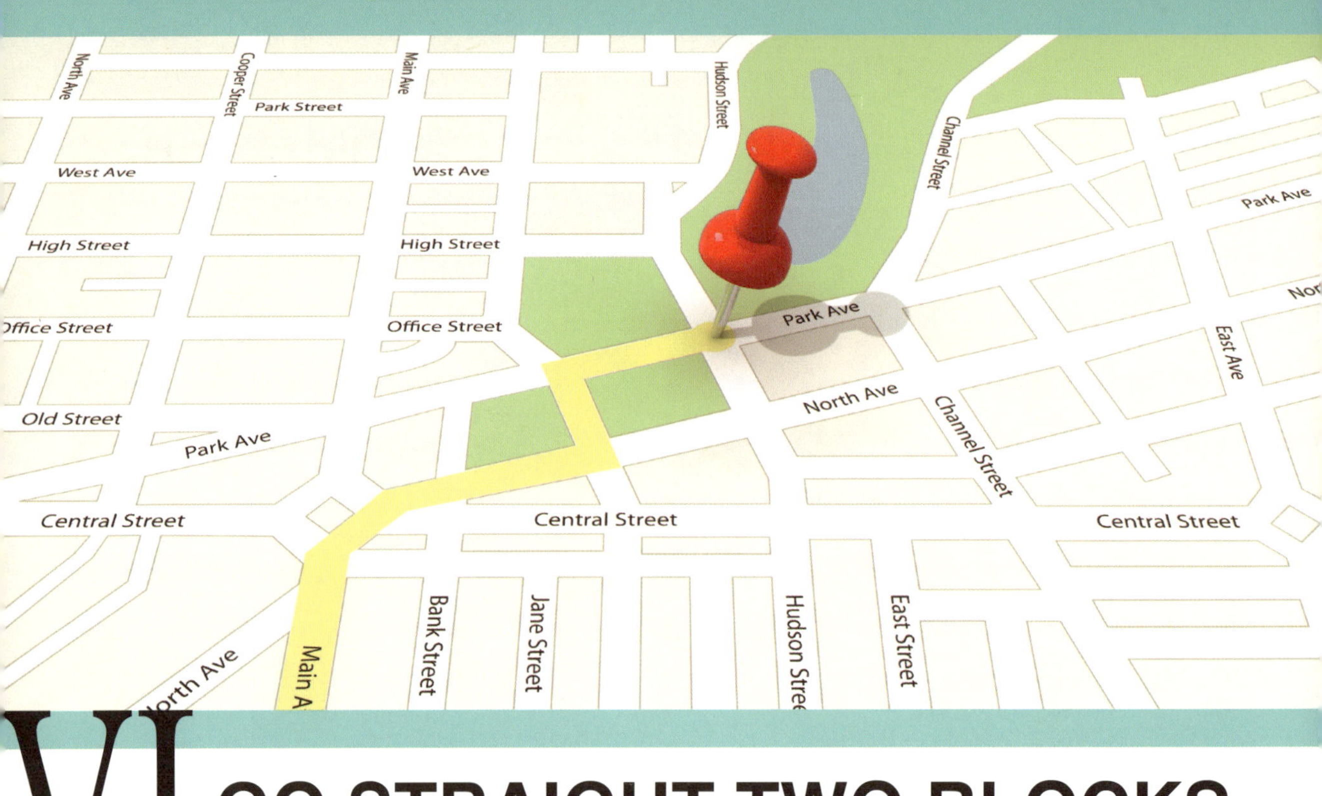

VI GO STRAIGHT TWO BLOCKS.

길 묻기

이 근처에 ∼이 있나요?	Is there ~ near here?
∼이 어디인지 아시나요?	Do you know where ~ is?
여기서 ∼에 어떻게 가면 되나요?	How can I get to ~ from here?
∼에 어떻게 가야 하는지 알려주시겠어요?	Could you show/tell me how to get to ~?

길 안내하기

직진하세요.	Go straight.
왼쪽으로 도세요.	Turn left. / Make a left turn.
그것은 ∼의 맞은편에 있어요.	It's across from ~.
그것은 ∼의 옆에 있어요.	It's next to ~.
그것은 여기서 그리 멀지 않아요.	It's not far from here.
찾기 쉬우실 거예요.	You can't miss it.

Words   *Direction*

- between
- beside
- east
- familiar
- head
- lost
- north
- reach
- south
- straight
- transfer
- west

01 대화를 듣고, 대화의 내용과 관계 있는 표지판을 고르세요.

a   b   c

02 대화를 듣고, a – c에 들어갈 말을 차례대로 써 넣으세요.

a 1st Stop: __________   **b** 2nd Stop: __________   **c** 3rd Stop: __________

03 주어진 표현을 사용하여 대화를 완성하세요.

You can't miss it	next to the gas station
Go down this street	Do you know where the supermarket is

A Oh, excuse me. _________________________________?

B Uh, sure. _____________________________ until you reach the bakery.

A Yes. And then?

B Turn right at the bakery and go down two more blocks. It is

_________________________. _________________________.

들려주는 내용을 잘 듣고 물음에 답하세요.

1 대화를 듣고, 남자가 이용할 교통 수단을 고르세요.

① ② ③ ④ ⑤

2 대화를 듣고, 남자가 찾고 있는 것을 고르세요.

① a desk
② a cell phone
③ a guest room
④ a public phone
⑤ a bathing suit

3 대화를 듣고, 화장실의 위치를 고르세요.

4 대화를 듣고, 여자의 마지막 말의 의미로 알맞은 것을 고르세요.

① 지리를 잘 모른다.
② 면접에 대해 들은 바 없다.
③ 면접을 잘 보길 바란다.
④ 10분 동안 시간을 낼 수 없다.
⑤ 남자가 찾고 있는 곳이 굉장히 멀다.

5 대화를 듣고, 이어질 두 사람의 행동으로 알맞은 것을 고르세요.

① 버스를 갈아탄다.
② Danny에게 길을 알려준다.
③ Danny와의 약속을 취소한다.
④ 행인에게 시간을 물어본다.
⑤ South Market으로 전화를 건다.

6 다음을 듣고, 이 안내방송을 들을 수 있는 장소를 고르세요.

① in a taxi   ② on a plane   ③ on a ship
④ on a train   ⑤ in a cable car

7 대화를 듣고, Baltimore Station에서 Hilton 호텔까지 어떻게 가야 하는지 고르세요.

① 지하철을 탄다.
② West Avenue로 간다.
③ 남쪽으로 가는 열차를 탄다.
④ 남쪽으로 세 정거장을 더 간다.
⑤ 북쪽으로 세 블록을 걸어 간다.

8 대화를 듣고, 여자의 말에 이어질 남자의 응답으로 알맞은 것을 고르세요.

M

① You can't miss it.
② I'm pleased to meet you.
③ Sorry, but I'm not good at computers.
④ It's on the second floor, next to the entrance.
⑤ You can use the computer lab anytime.

다음을 듣고 빈칸에 들어갈 알맞은 말을 쓰세요.

1

M Hey, Lisa, ________ ________ ________ ________ near here?

W Sure. Go up the street ________ ________ . It's ________ ________ ________ ________ of the Radio Station.

M Just five blocks? I don't have to ________ ________ ________ , then.

W Yeah, you can just ________ ________ ________ ________ there.

M That's exactly ________ ________ ________ to do.

2

M Sorry, but ________ ________ ________ ________ ?

W Of course. What is it?

M I ________ ________ ________ my cell phone and have to ________ ________ ________ . Is there ________ ________ ________ anywhere around here?

W There's one at the front desk ________ ________ ________ ________ . It's right ________ ________ ________ ________ .

M Oh, right! That's where ________ ________ ________ , too, right?

W ________ .

3

M Hey, honey, do you know where ________ ________ ________ ? I ________ ________ ________ on my shirt.

W Uh, yeah. ________ ________ and go past the roller coasters. Then ________ ________ and walk past the gift shop.

M So they're ________ ________ ________ ________ ?

W Yeah, between that and the snack stand.

4

M ________ ________ , miss. Could you help me ________ ________ ________ ________ ?

W Sure. ________ ________ ________ ________ ?

M Could you tell me where the Tyson Shipping Offices are? I have an interview ________ ________ ________ ________ there in ten minutes.

W Oh, sorry, but I'm not ________ ________ ________ ________ .

5

W _________ _________ _________ _________ for South Market?

M Yeah. We _________ _________ _________ in about 30 minutes.

W But _________ _________ _________ _________! We need to get there by 8:15. Danny will be waiting for us.

M Oh, we _________ _________ _________ bus 443, then.

W What? Isn't this bus 443?

M No, _________ _________ _________ 433.

W Oh, no! Hurry up. _________ _________ _________ at the next stop and transfer to bus 443.

M OK.

6

W Good afternoon, ladies and gentlemen. _________ _________ _________ _________ _________. Our plane is _________ _________ _________ in New York at 6:30 p.m. This will be a _________ _________. We _________ _________ _________ at 4:00 p.m., and we will start our in-flight movie at 4:30 p.m. If you have any other questions, please _________ _________ _________ _________. Thank you.

7

W Hey, can you tell me _________ _________ _________ to the Hilton Hotel?

M Yeah. _________ _________ _________ to the West Avenue station. Then take the Southbound train to Baltimore Station. From there _________ _________ _________ to the hotel.

W Okay. How far _________ _________ _________ is it?

M It's _________ _________ _________.

W Thank you very much.

8

M Hey, _________ _________ _________. Do you need some help?

W Oh, yes, please. I'm _________ _________ _________ _________, so I don't know where anything is.

M Where do you _________ _________ _________?

W I want to know where _________ _________ _________ _________.

I'M PRETTY GOOD AT IT.

UNIT VII

가능성 묻기

~을 할 수 있나요?	Can you ~?
~을 하는 방법을 아세요?	Do you know how to ~?

가능 표현하기

물론 가능합니다.	Sure, I can.
문제 없어요.	No problem.
나는 ~을 꽤 잘해요.	I'm pretty good at ~.

불가능 표현하기

미안하지만 할 수 없어요.	Sorry, but I can't.
그건 불가능해요.	That's impossible.
난 ~을 어떻게 하는지 몰라요.	I have no idea how to ~.

Words **Sports**

 active  compete  fair  kick  lose  match

 outdoor  skill  stadium tackle teamwork throw

 대화를 듣고, 어제와 오늘, 내일의 날씨를 순서대로 배열하세요.

______ → ______ → ______

02 대화를 듣고, Jessica가 할 수 있는 운동에 모두 ✓ 표 하세요.

a Tennis ☐
b Badminton ☐
c Swimming ☐

03 주어진 표현을 사용하여 대화를 완성하세요.

I have no idea	I'm not good at making
could possibly help you	Do you know how to make

A _____________________ a computer program?

B Uh, not really. _____________________ computer programs.

A Aw. I want to make a program for a video game, but _____________________ how to begin.

B You know, I have a friend who's good at that stuff. He _____________________ .

들려주는 내용을 잘 듣고 물음에 답하세요.

1 대화를 듣고, 여자가 토요일 오전에 하는 일을 고르세요.

①   ②   ③   ④   ⑤

2 다음 중 어색한 대화를 고르세요.

①   ②   ③   ④   ⑤

3 대화를 듣고, 남자가 여자에게 부탁한 일을 고르세요.

① 토요일에 동아리 활동을 도와줄 것
② 여행 일정을 연기해 줄 것
③ 함께 해변에 가 줄 것
④ 함께 동아리 가입을 해 줄 것
⑤ 다음 주에 3일 더 동아리 활동을 할 것

4 대화를 듣고, 두 사람의 관계로 알맞은 것을 고르세요.

① 아버지 – 딸   ② 코치 – 운동 선수   ③ 교장 – 교사
④ 기자 – 운동 선수   ⑤ 의사 – 환자

5 다음을 듣고, 글의 종류가 무엇인지 고르세요.

① an invitation   ② a notice   ③ an advertisement
④ a letter   ⑤ a news story

6 대화를 듣고, 여자의 결혼식 날짜를 고르세요.

June						
Sun	Mon	Tue	Wed	Thu	Fri	Sat
	1	2	3	4	5	6
7	8	9	10	11	12	13
14	15	16	17	18	19	20
21	22	23	24	25	26	27
28	29	30				

① 19일   ② 20일   ③ 21일   ④ 27일   ⑤ 28일

7 대화를 듣고, 남자의 마지막 말의 의도를 고르세요.

① 기대   ② 충고   ③ 사과   ④ 항의   ⑤ 감사

8 다음을 듣고, 수업의 규칙에 대해 언급되지 <u>않은</u> 내용을 고르세요.

① Students will write 3 papers.
② Students must not miss the class.
③ Students will do a group project.
④ Students will take a test every Friday.
⑤ Students must do homework every night.

다음을 듣고 빈칸에 들어갈 알맞은 말을 쓰세요.

1

M Hey, Clarice, do you want to ________ ________ ________ ________ with me on Wednesday night?

W Oh, sorry, Louis. I ________ ________ ________ that night.

M Oh, I see. Well ________ ________ ________ ________, then?

W I can't. I ________ ________ ________ early Saturday morning, so I ________ ________ ________ then.

M Oh. Well ________ ________ ________ ________ ________?

W Hmm. ________ ________ ________ Sunday afternoon.

2

① **W** Danny, ________ ________ ________? I want to learn how to ski.

  M Oh, yes, ________ ________ ________ ________.

② **W** Are you ________ ________ ________?

  M Yeah, I usually ________ ________ ________ ________ on math tests.

③ **W** Do you know ________ ________ ________ this fax machine?

  M Peggy said she will ________ ________ ________ ________.

④ **W** Can you make six dresses by Friday?

  M ________ ________. I need ________ ________ ________ ________ to do that.

⑤ **W** Do you think Mr. Black will fire Karen?

  M It's possible. She ________ ________ ________ ________ lately.

3

M Hey, Allison. Do you ________ ________ ________?

W Sure, Bill. ________ ________?

M Well, we're going to be really busy on Saturday. I was wondering if ________ ________ ________ ________ ________ to help.

W Uh, sorry, but I don't think I can. My sister and I are ________ ________ ________ ________ this weekend. Besides, ________ ________ ________ 3 extra days for our club this week.

M Oh, I didn't know that. ________ ________ ________ ________, then.

4

W ________ ________ ________ ________ ________, Mr. Baker?

M Sure. What is it, Helen?

W I feel like ________ ________ ________ yesterday because of me. I think ________ ________ ________.

M Oh, Helen. Don't say that. ________ ________ ________ ________.

W But ________ ________ ________ ________ volleyball at all.

Dictation

M That's not true. You are ________ ________ ________, and you've been
________ ________ ________ to our team.

5

M Today was a happy day in West Virginia. ________ ________ ________
________ from almost certain death. A week ago ________ ________ ________
inside the tunnel. They had ________ ________ ________ ________, and they
had ________ ________ ________ ________ ________. Fortunately, however,
________ ________ ________ ________. They have all returned to their
families, who never ________ ________ ________.

6

M Hey, Carol. I heard that ________ ________ ________. Congratulations!
W Oh, thank you, Dave. Can you ________ ________ ________ ________?
M When is it?
W It's the ________ ________ ________ ________.
M Sure, I can. I'll bring ________ ________ ________ for you.
W Thank you.

7

M Excuse me. Is ________ ________ ________ ________?
W Oh, yes, but ________ ________ ________ ________.
M What? Why?
W There's ________ ________ ________ at the pool today. Only invited guests are
allowed in. You'll have to ________ ________ ________ ________ ________
tomorrow.
M ________ ________ ________! I have to go to school tomorrow and I'll have to
wait ________ ________ ________ to go swimming!

8

W Good morning, everyone. Welcome to Freshman Chemistry. There are just
________ ________ ________ ________ for this course. First, you ________
________ ________ every night. Second, you will have a quiz or test every
Friday. You will also have to ________ ________ ________, and you will have
________ ________ ________. Don't worry, though. ________ ________
________ ________ ________, but it will not be impossible.

VIII HOW OFTEN DO YOU SWIM?

빈도 묻기와 답하기

당신은 얼마나 자주 ~을 하나요?
당신은 하루에 몇 번 ~을 하나요?
저는 보통 한 주에 한 번/두 번/
세 번 ~을 해요.

How often do you ~?
How many times do you ~ a day?
I usually ~ once/twice/three times
a week.

수량 묻기와 답하기

당신은 얼마나 많은 ~을 … 하나요?
몇 개의 오렌지를 원하나요?
전 여섯 개의 오렌지를 원해요.

How many ~ do you … ?
How many oranges do you want?
I want six oranges.

Words   **Entertainment**

amusement park　crowded　funny　exciting　expect
humorous　pleasant　relax　relieve　scary　stress
thrill

대화를 듣고, 남자와 여자가 좋아하는 영화 장르를 알맞게 연결하세요.

1

2

a

b

c

대화를 듣고, 내용과 일치하도록 괄호 안에서 알맞은 말을 고르세요.

1 The boy's favorite activity is (inline skating, swimming).
2 The girl goes swimming about (once a week, twice a month).

03

주어진 표현을 사용하여 대화를 완성하세요.

How many puppies	three times a day
I have eight puppies	How often do you feed them

A Peggy, I heard you have many puppies.
_______________________ do you have?
B _______________________.
A _______________________ a day?
B I feed them _______________________.

들려주는 내용을 잘 듣고 물음에 답하세요.

1 대화를 듣고, 남자가 주말에 한 일을 고르세요.

①　②　③　④　⑤

2 대화를 듣고, 남자가 한 달에 읽는 책의 권 수를 고르세요.

① 2권　② 5권　③ 10권　④ 15권　⑤ 20권

3 다음을 듣고, 여자의 심정으로 알맞은 것을 고르세요.

① excited　② relaxed　③ jealous
④ angry　⑤ satisfied

4 대화를 듣고, 이어서 들려주는 질문에 알맞은 답을 고르세요.

① once a week　② twice a week
③ three times a week　④ four times a week
⑤ five times a week

5 다음 중 그래프와 일치하지 <u>않는</u> 설명을 고르세요.

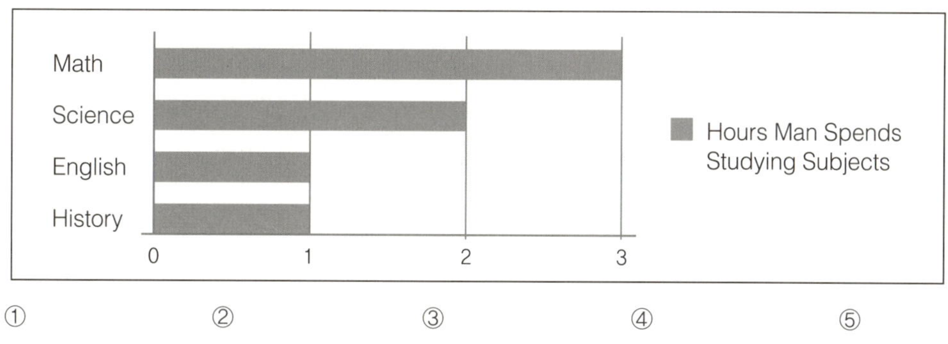

①   ②   ③   ④   ⑤

6 대화를 듣고, 여자가 남자를 찾아온 이유를 고르세요.

① 휴가 신청을 하기 위해   ② 실적을 보고하기 위해   ③ 조퇴를 허락받기 위해
④ 근무 시간을 변경하기 위해   ⑤ 급여 인상을 요구하기 위해

7 다음 그림의 상황에 맞는 대화를 고르세요.

①   ②   ③   ④   ⑤

8 대화를 듣고, 여자의 말에 이어질 남자의 응답으로 알맞은 것을 고르세요.

M ____

① I think you had a flat tire.
② The car broke down two days ago.
③ Did you fix the problem by yourself?
④ Sorry, but there's nothing I can do.
⑤ I'm not sure, but I don't think it'll take too long.

다음을 듣고 빈칸에 들어갈 알맞은 말을 쓰세요.

1

W Leo, did you ________ ________ ________ ________?
M Yeah, I had a good time with my girlfriend.
W ________ ________ ________ ________?
M I wanted to go ________ ________ ________ ________, but my girlfriend didn't want to. So we went to the new city zoo instead.
W ________ ________ ________?
M Yeah, but we had ________ ________ ________ ________. The best thing there was the panda bear.

2

M Oh, you have ________ ________ ________ ________, Kate!
W Yeah, I like to read, so I often ________ ________ ________ ________ and buy books.
M ________ ________ ________ do you read a month?
W ________ ________, I think.
M Really? You read ________ ________ ________ ________ as me.

3

W I can't believe this! I just ________ ________ ________ ________ at the airport, but I ________ ________ ________! There's a ________ ________ outside, and almost all the roads ________ ________. I've already waited for four hours for my dad to come pick me up. ________ ________ ________ will the wait be? I just want to get out of here and ________ ________ ________ ________.

4

M Hey, Claire! ________ ________ ________?
W I'm doing OK. Ryan. I didn't know ________ ________ ________.
M Yeah. I ________ ________ here.
W Really? ________ ________ ________ ________ here before. ________ ________ ________ ________ ________ ________?
M ________ ________ ________ ________. How about you?
W I come here ________ ________ ________.

5

M ① The man ________ ________ ________ ________ studying math.
  ② The man studies English and history ________ ________ ________ ________ of time.

③ The man ________ ________ ________ ________ studying science.
④ The man studies math for ________ ________ ________ ________.
⑤ The man studies history for ________ ________ two hours.

6

W Excuse me, Mr. Davis?

M Oh, good morning, Cathy. Come in. ________ ________ ________ ________?

W Well, sir, I was wondering if I could take ________ ________ ________ ________ next month.

M ________ ________ ________ would you like off?

W Three days, sir. From Wednesday, October 6th to Friday, October 8th.

M Okay.

7

① W What's the problem?

   M I have a ________ ________ and I ________ ________ ________.

② W Did you ________ ________ ________ ________?

   M Yes, I bought some medicine ________ ________ ________ ________.

③ W Let me take a look at your arm. ________ ________ ________?

   M Yes, I think ________ ________.

④ W Don't forget ________ ________ ________ ________ three times a day.

   M Okay, ________ ________.

⑤ W Hey, you look terrible. I think you should ________ ________ ________ ________.

   M Okay. Could you ________ ________ ________ ________ ________?

8

M ________ ________ ________ ________ you today, ma'am?

W It's my car. I was driving the other day, and ________ ________ ________ a lot.

M Did you have ________ ________ ________?

W No, the tires are fine. I think there may be something wrong ________ ________ ________.

M I see. We'll ________ ________ ________ ________ it.

W Thank you. ________ ________ ________ will it take to fix the problem?

IX YOU'D BETTER HURRY UP.

충고 요구하기

제가 ~해야 한다고 생각하시나요?	Do you think I should ~?
~하기 위해 제가 어떻게 해야 하죠?	What should I do to ~?

충고하기

넌 ~해야 해.	You should ~.
난 네가 ~해야 한다고 생각해.	I think you should ~.
너는 ~하는 (하지 않는) 편이 좋을 거야.	You'd better (not) ~.

충고에 답하기

좋은 생각이야.	That's a good idea. / That sounds good.
생각해 볼게.	I'll think about it.

Words **Jobs**

 apply    astronaut    astronomer    career    employ

 firefighter    job interview    job offer   lawyer   position

 professional   quit

01 대화를 듣고, 현재의 시각을 고르세요.

a

b

c

02 대화를 듣고, 아래에서 비디오 게임에 대한 Kevin과 Jean의 의견을 각각 골라 기호를 쓰세요.

---

a. 스트레스를 풀어준다.

b. 시간 낭비일 뿐이다.

c. 정신 건강에 좋지 않다.

d. 새로운 친구를 사귈 수 있게 해 준다.

---

1 Kevin: ________________   **2** Jean : ________________

03 주어진 표현을 사용하여 대화를 완성하세요.

You'd better exercise	That's a good idea
I think you should	what should I do

A Ron, ________________________ to lose weight?

B ________________________ stop eating junk food.

A Okay. And what else?

B ________________________ every day.

A ________________________. Thank you.

들려주는 내용을 잘 듣고 물음에 답하세요.

1 다음을 듣고, 내용과 관련된 직업을 고르세요.

①   ②   ③   ④   ⑤

   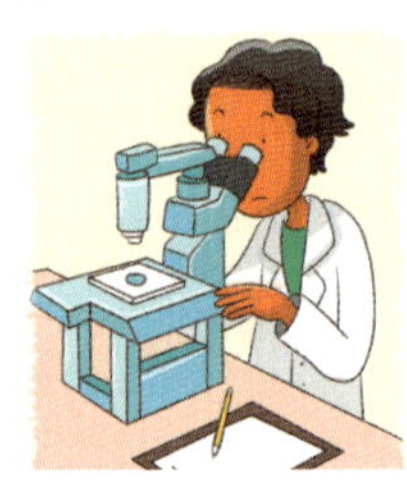 

2 대화를 듣고, 남자의 고민이 무엇인지 고르세요.

① 진로를 정하지 못했다.
② 성적이 점점 떨어지고 있다.
③ 금전적으로 여유가 없다.
④ 교우 관계가 원만하지 않다.
⑤ 부모님과 진학 문제로 갈등이 있다.

3 다음을 듣고, 메모된 내용 중 잘못된 것을 고르세요.

① To: Ms. Park
② From: Allen Smith
③ Reason: To change the time of the appointment
④ Meeting Time: 10:30 a.m., Friday
⑤ Place: Smith's office

4 다음 중 어색한 대화를 고르세요.

①   ②   ③   ④   ⑤

5 대화를 듣고, 관계 깊은 속담을 고르세요.

① A stitch in time saves nine.
② Look before you leap.
③ Every cloud has a silver lining.
④ A watched pot never boils.
⑤ A bad workman blames his tools.

6 대화를 듣고, 내용과 일치하는 것을 고르세요.

① Walter는 다음 주에 여행을 갈 것이다.
② Walter의 목적지는 New York이다.
③ Walter는 해외로 출장을 가게 되었다.
④ Walter는 이미 호텔 예약을 마쳤다.
⑤ Walter는 삼촌의 집에서 머물 수도 있다.

7 대화를 듣고, 여자가 남자에게 충고한 내용을 고르세요.

① 머리를 길러보아라.
② 외모에 더 신경을 써라.
③ 기분 전환을 해라.
④ 데이트 계획을 꼼꼼하게 짜 놓아라.
⑤ 여자들과 대화를 많이 해 보아라.

8 대화를 듣고, 여자의 말에 이어질 남자의 응답으로 알맞은 것을 고르세요.

M

① Don't mention it.
② I'm really happy for you.
③ I'm sorry to hear that.
④ That's a good idea. I'll do that.
⑤ I'm sorry that she can't come.

다음을 듣고 빈칸에 들어갈 알맞은 말을 쓰세요.

1

M To get this job, you should get __________ __________ __________ __________
__________. You should be very __________ __________ __________ if you want to
do it. You also need to study a lot of __________ __________ and learn how to fly
__________ __________. It is a very difficult job. That's why __________ __________
__________ __________ it.

2

M Ms. Ellen? I __________ __________ __________.
W Sure Paul. What's on your mind?
M All my friends have a dream, but I have no idea what I want to do __________
__________ __________ __________.
W Paul, you're only 15. __________ __________ __________ __________.
M Yeah, but I'd still like some ideas.
W Well, you're __________ __________ __________, and you're very smart. I think you
should __________ __________ __________.
M That's something to think about. Thanks.

3

M Hello, Ms. Park? This is Allen Smith. I am __________ __________ __________ from
yesterday. I am honored that your magazine __________ __________ __________
__________. If you like, you can interview me at my office __________ __________
this Friday. You should get here earlier than that, though. It can be difficult to
__________ __________ __________ __________ here after 9:00. I hope __________
__________ __________ then!

4

① M I have __________ __________ __________.
　 W I think you should __________ __________ __________.
② M I lost my brother's favorite book. __________ __________ __________ __________?
　 W __________ __________ __________ __________ with him.
③ M Do you think I should __________ __________ __________?
　 W Well, I think __________ __________ __________ __________ __________.
④ M What should I do __________ __________ __________?
　 W I think you can do well.
⑤ M __________ __________ __________ stay up all night.
　 W Yeah, I think you're right.

5

W Thomas. ___________ ___________ __________. What's wrong?

M __________ __________ __________ __________. It's painful.

W Oh, that's too bad. I think you should __________ __________ __________ __________
right away.

M It will be OK. __________ __________ __________.

W Thomas, if you don't go see a dentist now, the problem will keep __________
__________ __________ __________. You might have to pull the tooth out.

M Yeah, you're right.

6

W Hey, Walter. How's it going?

M __________ __________ __________ __________ today. I just __________ __________
__________ __________ to New Orleans for next month.

W Oh, cool! Are you going to the big festival there?

M I sure am. I just need to __________ __________ __________ to stay in.

W Yeah, you'd better __________ __________ __________ as soon as possible.
Otherwise, you __________ __________ __________ __________ __________ in time.

M I know, I know. If I can't, it's no problem, though. I can stay __________ __________
__________ __________ there.

7

W Hey, Mitch, __________ __________ __________. What's the problem?

M I asked Sandra out on a date, but she said no. I __________ __________ __________.

W I have an idea. It could be the way you look.

M __________ __________ __________ how I look?

W Well, it's just that you'll be popular with girls if you __________ __________ __________
__________. For example, I think you should get a nice haircut.

M Well, I could __________ __________ __________ __________.

8

W Hey, Jason? Peggy's birthday is this Friday.

M Oh. It is?

W Yeah. She's having __________ __________ __________ and she wants you to come.
__________ __________ __________ __________?

M I'm afraid I can't. I already __________ __________ __________.

W Well, that's too bad. __________ __________ __________ __________ and wish her a
happy birthday, though. I'm sure __________ __________ __________.

X ARE YOU INTERESTED IN ART?

관심 묻기

너는 ~을 좋아하니?	Do you enjoy ~?
너는 ~에 관심이 있니?	Are you interested in ~?
너는 무엇에 관심이 있니?	What are you interested in?

관심, 무관심 말하기

나는 ~을 즐겨 해.	I enjoy ~.
나는 ~에 관심이 있어.	I'm interested in ~.
나는 ~에 관심이 별로 없어.	I don't have much interest in ~.

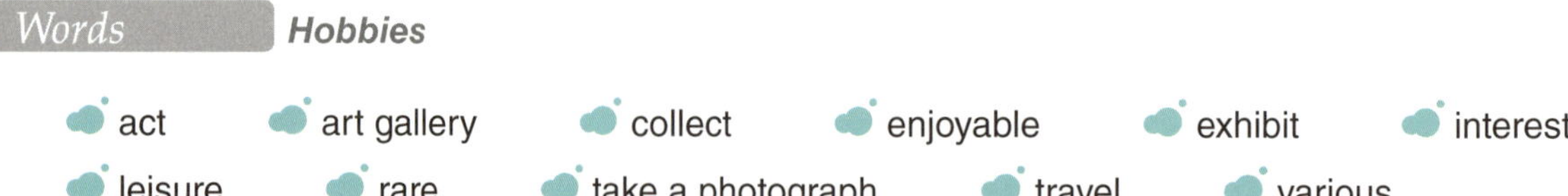

Words **Hobbies**

- act
- art gallery
- collect
- enjoyable
- exhibit
- interest
- leisure
- rare
- take a photograph
- travel
- various

01 대화를 듣고, 두 사람이 주말에 할 일을 고르세요.

02 대화를 듣고, 언급된 내용에 모두 ✓ 표 하세요.

a Jeremy는 연기를 하고 싶어 한다. ☐

b Jeremy는 연극부에 가입했다. ☐

c Jeremy는 다음 주 수요일에 오디션을 볼 것이다. ☐

03 주어진 표현을 사용하여 대화를 완성하세요.

are you interested in	What are you interested in
I am interested in pop music	don't have much interest in

A Ron, _______________________ rock music?

B Oh, sorry, but I _______________________ rock.

A _______________________ then?

B _______________________, and my favorite singer is Mariah Carey.

들려주는 내용을 잘 듣고 물음에 답하세요.

1 다음 그림의 상황에 맞는 대화를 고르세요.

①   ②   ③   ④   ⑤

2 대화를 듣고, 대화의 주제를 고르세요.

① 좋아하는 영화 장르
③ 영화 보기에 좋은 장소
⑤ 영화 장르에 대한 남녀의 인식 차이

② 로맨틱 코미디 영화의 장점
④ 영화 감상의 바른 자세

3 대화를 듣고, 남자가 도서관에 자주 가지 않는 이유를 고르세요.

① 책 읽기를 싫어해서
③ 도서관에 자료가 별로 없어서
⑤ 도서관이 일찍 문을 닫아서

② 도서관이 너무 멀어서
④ 도서관에 사람이 너무 많아서

4 대화를 듣고, 여자의 말에 이어질 남자의 응답으로 알맞은 것을 고르세요.

M ______________________________________

① Thanks. That would be a great help.
② What does your uncle look like?
③ Sorry, but I don't think I can.
④ You'd better follow his advice.
⑤ I hope your dreams come true.

5 대화를 듣고, 내용과 일치하는 것을 고르세요.

① 여자는 어제 축구 경기를 보았다.
② 남자는 스포츠를 싫어한다.
③ 여자는 뮤지컬 관람을 좋아한다.
④ 남자는 뮤지컬을 싫어한다.
⑤ 여자는 남자의 제안을 거절했다.

6 대화를 듣고, 남자가 지불해야 할 금액을 고르세요.

ON SALE TODAY

Shirt:	$25
Sweater:	$50
Pants:	$30
Shoes:	$50

① $55　　② $80　　③ $100　　④ $110　　⑤ $130

7 대화를 듣고, 이어서 들려주는 질문에 알맞은 답을 고르세요.

① singing
② playing soccer
③ playing the guitar
④ listening to jazz
⑤ writing songs

8 대화를 듣고, 여자의 의견을 고르세요.

① Cats are good pets.
② Dogs need a lot of care.
③ Dogs are better than cats.
④ Any pet can be a person's best friend.
⑤ Keeping a pet is not a good idea.

다음을 듣고 빈칸에 들어갈 알맞은 말을 쓰세요.

1

① W　Hey, do you know ＿＿＿＿＿ ＿＿＿＿＿ ＿＿＿＿＿ ＿＿＿＿＿ are?

　　M　＿＿＿＿＿ ＿＿＿＿＿ ＿＿＿＿＿ ＿＿＿＿＿.

② W　Wow. There are ＿＿＿＿＿ ＿＿＿＿＿ ＿＿＿＿＿ here.

　　M　Yeah, I don't know ＿＿＿＿＿ ＿＿＿＿＿ ＿＿＿＿＿ ＿＿＿＿＿.

③ W　＿＿＿＿＿ ＿＿＿＿＿ ＿＿＿＿＿. Let's go outside.

　　M　Oh, but it's too hot outside. ＿＿＿＿＿ ＿＿＿＿＿ ＿＿＿＿＿ ＿＿＿＿＿.

④ W　Are you interested ＿＿＿＿＿ ＿＿＿＿＿ ＿＿＿＿＿ ＿＿＿＿＿, dear?

　　M　No. I heard it wasn't that good.

⑤ W　Ted, ＿＿＿＿＿ ＿＿＿＿＿ this tennis club.

　　M　Well, I'm not really ＿＿＿＿＿ ＿＿＿＿＿ ＿＿＿＿＿.

2

W　Hey, Edward, are you ＿＿＿＿＿ ＿＿＿＿＿ ＿＿＿＿＿ a romantic comedy?

M　What? No, I ＿＿＿＿＿ ＿＿＿＿＿ ＿＿＿＿＿.

W　You do? I love them. They are ＿＿＿＿＿ ＿＿＿＿＿ ＿＿＿＿＿ ＿＿＿＿＿ ＿＿＿＿＿.

M　Not for me. I think ＿＿＿＿＿ ＿＿＿＿＿ ＿＿＿＿＿.

W　＿＿＿＿＿ ＿＿＿＿＿ ＿＿＿＿＿ ＿＿＿＿＿ do you like to watch then?

M　I enjoy watching ＿＿＿＿＿ ＿＿＿＿＿ ＿＿＿＿＿.

3

M　Hey, Dora. ＿＿＿＿＿ ＿＿＿＿＿ ＿＿＿＿＿ studying in the library?

W　Actually, I do. It's ＿＿＿＿＿ ＿＿＿＿＿ ＿＿＿＿＿ in there. And all those books ＿＿＿＿＿ ＿＿＿＿＿ ＿＿＿＿＿.

M　Hmm. Well, I don't study in there often.

W　Why?

M　I ＿＿＿＿＿ ＿＿＿＿＿ ＿＿＿＿＿ at night to study, and the library ＿＿＿＿＿ ＿＿＿＿＿ ＿＿＿＿＿ for me.

W　I don't think that's ＿＿＿＿＿ ＿＿＿＿＿ ＿＿＿＿＿ ＿＿＿＿＿.

4

W　Danny, what are you reading?

M　It's an article about ＿＿＿＿＿ ＿＿＿＿＿ ＿＿＿＿＿ ＿＿＿＿＿.

W　Oh, ＿＿＿＿＿ ＿＿＿＿＿ ＿＿＿＿＿ in medicine?

M　Yeah, I really am. I want to ＿＿＿＿＿ ＿＿＿＿＿ ＿＿＿＿＿ when I'm older. But I don't really know ＿＿＿＿＿ ＿＿＿＿＿ ＿＿＿＿＿ to become one.

W　Actually, my uncle is a doctor. I can ask him ＿＿＿＿＿ ＿＿＿＿＿ ＿＿＿＿＿ ＿＿＿＿＿ ＿＿＿＿＿, if you'd like.

5

M Did you see the soccer game last night?

W Uh, _________ _________ _________ _________ soccer. In fact, I don't like sports at all.

M Really? Well, _________ _________ _________ _________ _________?

W I really like _________ _________ _________ and plays with my friends. I _________ _________ _________.

M That's cool. Why don't we _________ _________ _________ _________ sometime?

W I'd love to.

6

W Are you interested in _________ _________ _________ _________, Harold?

M No, I'm not interested in shoes. I _________ _________ _________ _________. I do need to get _________ _________ _________ _________ pants, though.

W Okay. How about some shirts?

M Uh, yeah. I should _________ _________ _________ _________.

W Hey, check out this sweater! It feels really _________ _________ _________.

M But I don't like its color, and I don't think _________ _________ _________. Let's go.

7

W Darren, are you going to the soccer game Friday night?

M Oh, no. I'm not _________ _________ _________. And I have plans on Friday. This really good jazz band's _________ _________ _________ at the Cotton Lounge.

W Oh. Are you interested _________ _________ _________?

M Yeah. I _________ _________ _________ _________ about four years ago.

8

M Rebecca, I just _________ _________ _________ _________! She is so cute.

W Uh, _________ _________.

M Are you interested in _________ _________ _________?

W Uh, _________ _________. I'm not really interested in cats.

M What? _________ _________?

W I just don't think they make good pets. _________ _________ _________. They are very loyal and friendly, and _________ _________ _________ _________, too.

XI WHY DON'T YOU START JOGGING?

제안하고 답하기

~하는 것이 어떠니?

Why don't you ~? / How about ~?
What about ~?

물론이지. / 좋은 생각이야.

Sure. / That's a good idea. / Why not?

그렇게 하고 싶지만, 할 수 없어.

I'd love to, but I can't.

약속 시간과 장소 정하기

우리 몇 시에 만날까?

What time shall we make it?

5시에 만나자.

Let's meet at five o'clock.

10시에 만날 수 있니?

Can you make it at ten?

우리 어디에서 만날까?

Where shall we meet?

Words   *Exercise*

- aerobic
- fitness
- improve
- jog
- keep in good shape
- lose weight
- muscle
- out of shape
- physical
- regular
- stretch
- work out

01 대화를 듣고, 여자가 디저트로 선택한 음식을 고르세요.

a

b

02 대화를 듣고, 내용과 일치하도록 보기에서 알맞은 말을 골라 써넣으세요.

shop online	find a good gift
visit a department store	afford to buy a gift

1 The boy's problem is that he can't ___________________.
2 The girl suggests that the boy ___________________.

03 주어진 표현을 사용하여 대화를 완성하세요.

I'd love to	How about tomorrow night
Let's meet at 7 p.m.	why don't we have a group study

A Derrick, ___________________ tonight?
B ___________________, but I have basketball practice tonight.
A ___________________? We can meet at my house.
B That's a good idea. ___________________.

들려주는 내용을 잘 듣고 물음에 답하세요.

1 대화를 듣고, 두 사람이 만나기로 한 시각을 고르세요.

① 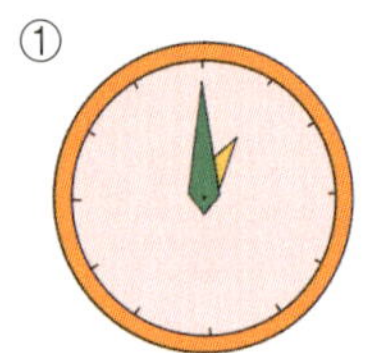 ②  ③ 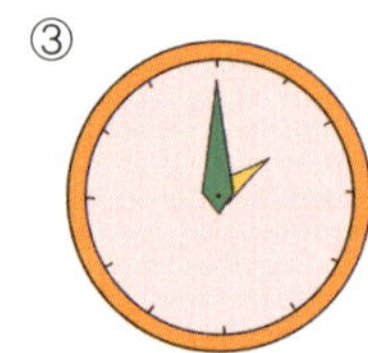 ④ 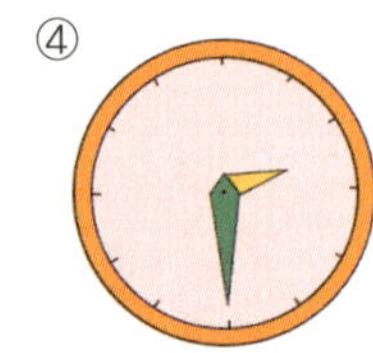 ⑤ 

2 대화를 듣고, 여자가 아들에게 한 조언을 고르세요.

① 산책을 해라.　　　② 잠깐 낮잠을 자라.　　　③ 숙제를 빨리 끝내라.
④ 몸을 따뜻이 해라.　　　⑤ 두통약을 먹어라.

3 다음을 듣고, 이어서 들려주는 질문에 알맞은 답을 고르세요.

① Saturday morning　　　② Saturday night　　　③ Sunday morning
④ Sunday night　　　⑤ Monday morning

4 대화를 듣고, 대화의 내용과 일치하지 <u>않는</u> 것을 고르세요.

① 현재 비가 오고 있다.
② 두 사람은 지하철을 기다리고 있다.
③ 두 사람의 목적지는 레스토랑이다.
④ 남자는 걸어갈 것을 제안한다.
⑤ 여자는 버스를 탔어야 했다고 후회한다.

5 대화를 듣고, 남자와 여자가 만날 장소를 고르세요.

6 대화를 듣고, 남자가 여자의 제안을 거절한 이유를 고르세요.

① 돈이 부족해서
② 운동을 싫어해서
③ 헬스장의 거리가 멀어서
④ 건강이 안 좋아져서
⑤ 운동을 할 시간이 없어서

7 대화를 듣고, 남자의 말에 이어질 여자의 응답으로 알맞은 것을 고르세요.

> W ______________________________________

① I don't really like action movies.
② Sure. I'd love to go see a movie, too.
③ What time shall we make it?
④ Because I'm not really hungry now.
⑤ Sorry, but I have to be home in 30 minutes.

8 다음을 듣고, 여자의 주장을 고르세요.

① 환경을 위해 나무를 많이 심자.
② 새 건물의 안전성을 다시 한 번 점검하자.
③ 새 건물을 짓는 것은 꼭 필요하다.
④ 목재 건물을 짓는 것이 비용이 적게 든다.
⑤ 새 건물을 짓는 대신 낡은 건물을 보수하자.

다음을 듣고 빈칸에 들어갈 알맞은 말을 쓰세요.

1

W Hello, is Mr. Gibson there?

M This is Mr. Gibson. How ______________ ______________ ______________ ______________?

W This is Amanda Preston. I'm with Carter Industries, and I'd like to ______________ ______________ ______________ ______________ ______________ with you.

M Oh, great! What time ______________ ______________ ______________?

W Any time after 1:00 p.m. on Wednesday would be best for me.

M Well, ______________ ______________ ______________?

W Okay. The interview will ______________ ______________ ______________ ______________. I'll meet you then.

2

W Brian, are you ______________ ______________ ______________ today?

M No, Mom, I still feel kind of sick. I ______________ ______________ ______________, but my head still hurts.

W Why don't you try ______________ ______________ ______________ for a while? It might ______________ ______________ ______________ more quickly.

M I wish I could. But I have to ______________ ______________ ______________ ______________.

3

M Hey Maria, it's Nick. I'm in town for the weekend. ______________ ______________ ______________ ______________ sometime? We can do something ______________ ______________ ______________. Sunday afternoon is free, too, but ______________ ______________ ______________ ______________. Just let me know ______________ ______________ ______________ we should meet. Please call me back ______________ ______________ ______________ this message. Thanks, bye.

4

W Jim, it's already 5:15. ______________ ______________ ______________ ______________ our second train will arrive?

M ______________ ______________ ______________ ______________. It should have arrived by now.

W Oh, we should have taken a bus ______________ ______________ ______________ ______________.

M Well, the restaurant is only a few blocks away now. ______________ ______________ ______________ ______________ the rest of the way?

W I think ______________ ______________ ______________ ______________.

M I guess you're right.

5

M Some of us are going out for pizza after work. _________ _________ _________ _________, Debbie?

W _________ _________? I haven't eaten all day. _________ _________ _________ _________?

M I know this great place called The Magic Mushroom.

W Hmm. I've never heard of it. _________ _________ _________ _________ _________?

M Okay. _________ _________ on Park Street, past the mall. Turn right _________ _________ _________ _________, and then _________ _________ on the first street.

W So it's on this street?

M Yeah. _________ _________ on the right.

6

M Oh, I'm so _________ _________ _________. I need to start exercising.

W How about _________ _________ _________? They have all kinds of machines and exercise programs there. At my gym, _________ _________ _________ $15 a month.

M Hmm. That's not _________ _________ _________. Where do you go?

W Great Fitness Gym over in Huntsville.

M Well, _________ _________ _________ from my house. I think I'll _________ _________ _________.

7

M So, what did you think about the movie?

W I _________ _________ _________. What about you?

M Well, I liked the story, but I didn't think _________ _________ _________ _________ _________.

W Yeah, _________ _________.

M Hey, _________ _________ _________? Why don't we _________ _________ for some dinner?

8

W I'd like to thank everyone _________ _________ _________. This meeting is about the city's new office complex. Many trees _________ _________ _________ _________ for this new building. It will also cost _________ _________ _________. Why don't we _________ _________ _________ on something else? We could use it to repair _________ _________ _________ _________ instead.

XII

WHAT DOES THAT MEAN?

표현 묻기

그건 무슨 뜻이죠?	What does that mean?
~일 때는 뭐라고 해야 하나요?	What should I say when ~?
~의 철자는 어떻게 되나요?	How do you spell ~?
이 문장이 옳은 문장인가요?	Is this sentence correct?

수정하기

미안하지만, 그건 틀렸어.	Sorry, but it's not right.
	I'm afraid it is wrong.
너는 실수를 했구나.	You've made a mistake.
이런/다른 방식으로 설명해 볼게.	Let me put it this/another way.

Words　　*Driving*

- blocked
- crash
- driver's license
- have a car accident
- have a flat tire
- limit
- safely
- slow down
- speeding ticket
- traffic jam
- traffic light
- wreck

 대화를 듣고, 현재 상황을 잘 나타낸 그림을 고르세요.

02 대화를 듣고, 여자의 충고로 알맞은 것을 고르세요.

a To use the Internet ☐
b To check his spelling ☐
c To use a dictionary ☐

03 주어진 표현을 사용하여 대화를 완성하세요.

How do you spell it	I'm afraid that's wrong
does this sentence mean	What does "provide" mean

A Mary, ________________________ "I'm sorry?"
B ________________________. It means "Thank you."
A One more question. ________________________?
B It means "to give."
A ________________________?
B P-r-o-v-i-d-e.

들려주는 내용을 잘 듣고 물음에 답하세요.

1 대화를 듣고, 남자의 현재 상황을 잘 나타낸 그림을 고르세요.

①  ②  ③  ④  ⑤ 

2 대화를 듣고, 내용과 일치하는 것을 고르세요.

① 남자는 자동차를 구입했다.
② 남자의 부모님은 자동차를 가지고 있다.
③ 남자는 운전 면허증 시험에 떨어졌다.
④ 남자는 운전 면허증 시험을 본 적이 없다.
⑤ 남자는 가지고 있던 자동차를 팔 것이다.

3 대화를 듣고, 남자가 언급한 'bumper to bumper'의 의미를 고르세요.

① 길을 잃었다.　　　② 교통체증이 심하다.　　　③ 말실수를 한다.
④ 자동차가 고장 났다.　　　⑤ 건망증이 심하다.

4 대화를 듣고, 남자가 기뻐하는 이유를 고르세요.

① 성적이 올라서
② 봉사활동을 해서
③ 학급의 반장이 되어서
④ 장학금을 받고 유학 가서
⑤ 미국 여행을 가게 되어서

5 다음 중 어색한 대화를 고르세요.

①   ②   ③   ④   ⑤

6 대화를 듣고, 여자의 말에 이어질 남자의 응답으로 알맞은 것을 고르세요.

> M ____

① Three times a week.   ② Yeah, I think so too.
③ I finished it last Sunday.   ④ I'm writing about World War II.
⑤ It's due this Friday.

7 다음을 듣고, 목차의 내용이 잘못된 것을 고르세요.

BIOLOGY

Table of Contents
① Chapter 1 – Food and Digestion
② Chapter 2 – Breathing
③ Chapter 3 – The Heart
④ Chapter 4 – Bones
⑤ Chapter 5 – Disease

8 다음을 듣고, 내용과 일치하지 <u>않는</u> 것을 고르세요.

① Highway 75 is now closed.
② Three cars were involved in the crash.
③ Only one person died in the accident.
④ Several people were taken to the hospital.
⑤ Traffic slowed down because of the accident.

다음을 듣고 빈칸에 들어갈 알맞은 말을 쓰세요.

1

W Hello, is Jeremy there?

M Hi, Samantha. This is Jeremy.

W Hey, I'm so sorry about __________ __________ __________. How bad were you hurt?

M Well, I have __________ __________ __________.

W "Fractured?" What __________ __________ __________ __________?

M It means "broken." I have to __________ __________ __________ for the next month.

W Oh, I'm sorry.

2

M Yes! This is __________ __________ __________!

W You mean __________ __________ __________?

M That's right. I finally got __________ __________ __________! Now all I need is a car.

W Didn't you say your parents would give you __________ __________ __________?

M Yeah. All I had to do was __________ __________ __________ __________. And I did! __________ __________ __________ to start driving everywhere.

W __________ __________ __________!

3

M Hey, Rachel. __________ __________ __________ __________.

W Oh. Kevin. What made you so late? __________ __________ __________ __________ about you.

M Oh, it was __________ __________ __________ out there.

W __________ __________ __________ __________ __________ "bumper to bumper?"

M It means that there is __________ __________ __________.

W Oh, I see.

4

M You'll never believe this.

W __________ __________ __________ __________? Do you have good news?

M The principal tells me I can study in America with __________ __________ __________! This is __________ __________ __________ __________!

W Wow! That's wonderful, dear! __________ __________ __________ for you. When do you go?

M Next month. Oh, __________ __________ __________ __________!

Dictation

5

① **M** Do you know what _________ _________ _________?

  W I have no idea.

② **M** What should I say when I want _________ _________ _________ _________?

  W Not at all. _________ _________.

③ **M** Daisy, is this sentence correct?

  W Well, I'm afraid _________ _________ _________.

④ **M** Kate, _________ _________ _________ _________ there. The spelling isn't right.

  W Oh, _________ _________ _________ _________ _________ then?

⑤ **M** I don't understand _________ _________ _________.

  W Well, _________ _________ _________ _________ another way.

6

W Jiwon, I think _________ _________ _________ _________. This spelling is incorrect.

M Really? _________ _________ _________ _________ "invasion?"

W I-n-v-a-s-i-o-n.

M Oh, thanks.

W Is that the paper for _________ _________ _________?

M Yeah. It's driving me crazy! _________ _________ _________ on this paper for a week, and I've still got _________ _________ _________ to write.

W Oh. _________ _________ _________ _________ _________ turn it in?

7

W OK, class, take out your new biology textbooks. Please turn to the Table of Contents. This will show you _________ _________ _________ _________ this semester. The first chapter is about food and digestion, and the second is _________ _________. After that, we take Test 1 and move on to Chapters 3 and 4. Chapter 3 is about the heart and 4 _________ _________ _________ _________. After this we take Test 2. After Test 2 we move on to Chapter 5, _________ _________ _________ _________.

8

M Now for _________ _________ _________. There is a _________ _________ _________ on Highway 75. Three cars crashed into each other. _________ _________ _________ in the accident, and they were taken to the hospital. The accident _________ _________ all traffic on the road. The road is now closed. This has _________ _________ _________ everywhere.

Memo

Memo

Memo

Memo

Answer & Script

감성 맞춤 내신 공략

센치한
Listening
길들이기

내신 만점을 향한 중등 영어 듣기 기본서

● 최신 개정 교육과정 분석 및 필수 의사소통 기능 수록
● 실제 영어 듣기평가와 가장 가까운 문제 유형 및 소재 제시
● 효과적인 1일 학습량 제시
● 다시 한 번 확인하는 Dictation 코너
● 시 · 도 교육청 듣기평가 대비 실전 모의고사 3회 수록

도약 1

Actual Test   **1** ⑤   **2** ①   **3** ③   **4** ④   **5** ③   **6** ④   **7** ②   **8** ① | p.08

1

M Hey, Deborah. Is something wrong?	**남** Deborah. 뭐가 잘못됐니?
W Yeah. I can't find my car keys anywhere.	**여** 응. 어디서도 자동차 열쇠를 찾을 수가 없어.
M Oh no! Where did you have them last?	**남** 이런! 마지막으로 어디에 두었는데?
W I put them in my coat pocket, but they fell out somewhere. I thought they fell out on the couch, but they were not there, either.	**여** 내 코트 주머니에 넣었는데 어딘가에 떨어졌어. 소파 위에 떨어졌다고 생각했는데 그 곳에도 없어.
M Oh, here! They were lying under the table.	**남** 아, 여기 봐! 탁자 아래에 놓여 있어.
W Thank you for helping me find them.	**여** 열쇠 찾는 걸 도와줘서 고마워.

2

[The telephone rings.]	[전화벨 소리]
W Hello?	**여** 여보세요?
M Hi, Annette. It's Phillip.	**남** 안녕, Annette. 나 Phillip이야.
W Oh, Phillip! It's been a while. How have you been?	**여** 아. Phillip! 오랜만이야. 어떻게 지냈니?
M I'm doing OK. I heard that you got married recently.	**남** 잘 지내고 있어. 난 네가 최근에 결혼했다는 소식을 들었어.
W Yeah, I got married to Arnold last month.	**여** 응. 난 지난 달에 Arnold와 결혼했어.
M Excellent! I'm happy to hear that. I wish you both the best.	**남** 잘됐구나! 그 말을 들으니 기뻐. 너희 두 사람이 행복하길 빌어.
W I appreciate that.	**여** 정말 고마워.

3

W Tim, I'd like to speak with you.	**여** Tim. 이야기를 좀 하고 싶구나.
M Sure, Mrs. Jenner. Is there a problem?	**남** 물론이죠. Jenner 선생님. 무슨 문제라도 있나요?
W Oh, not at all. I thought you did well on your presentation the other day.	**여** 아, 그렇지 않아. 난 네가 지난 번에 발표를 정말 잘했다고 생각했단다.
M Thanks for saying that. I worked really hard on it.	**남** 그렇게 말씀해주셔서 감사해요. 발표 준비를 정말 열심히 했었거든요.

W I know. The other students should <u>follow</u> your <u>example</u>. Again, <u>well done</u>.	**여** 알고 있단다. 다른 학생들도 너를 본받아야 할 거야. 다시 한 번 말하는데, 정말 훌륭했어.
M My pleasure.	**남** 기쁘군요.

Vocabulary	problem 문제 presentation 발표 the other day 지난 번에 follow one's example ~을 본받다

4

M Excuse me. I'd like to <u>borrow the new novel</u> by Stephen King. Do you have <u>any copies of it</u>?	**남** 실례합니다. 저는 Stephen King의 새 소설을 빌리고 싶습니다. 그 책이 있나요?
W Yes, sir. It's in the fiction section.	**여** 네. 소설 코너에 있습니다.
M <u>Where is that</u>?	**남** 어디인가요?
W It's at the front, <u>next to the movie</u> and magazine sections.	**여** 앞 쪽에 영화와 잡지 코너 옆에 있습니다.
M Thank you so much.	**남** 정말 감사합니다.
W Oh, <u>don't mention it</u>.	**여** 아, 천만에요.

Vocabulary	borrow 빌리다 novel 소설 copy (책) 한 부 fiction 소설, 허구 section 부문, 구획 front 앞 magazine 잡지

5

① **M** What is the problem, Susan?	① **남** 문제가 무엇이니, Susan?
W I think I <u>have a fever</u>.	**여** 제가 열이 나는 것 같아요.
② **M** The shirt looks <u>really good on you</u>.	② **남** 그 셔츠 네게 정말 잘 어울려.
W Thanks. <u>It's very nice of you</u> to say so.	**여** 고마워. 그렇게 말해주다니 친절하네.
③ **M** Okay, Samantha. I <u>removed that sore tooth</u>, so the pain will stop.	③ **남** 됐어, Samantha. 네 아픈 이를 뽑았으니 이제 통증이 없어질 거야.
W I'm grateful, Dr. Sheldon.	**여** 감사합니다. Sheldon 박사님.
④ **M** Well, I <u>fixed your engine</u>. Your car will run perfectly now.	④ **남** 음. 엔진을 수리했습니다. 차는 이제 완벽하게 잘 움직일 거에요.
W Thanks. <u>You did a good job</u>.	**여** 고마워요. 잘했군요.
⑤ **M** Nancy, I really <u>enjoyed your report</u> yesterday.	⑤ **남** Nancy, 난 어제 네 보고서를 정말 잘 읽었단다.
W Thanks. I'm glad <u>you liked it</u>, Mr. Taylor.	**여** 고맙습니다. 마음에 드셨다니 정말 기쁘네요, Taylor 선생님.

Vocabulary	have a fever 열이 나다 remove 제거하다 sore 아픈 tooth 이, 치아 pain 고통 fix 수리하다 engine 엔진 perfectly 완벽하게 report 보고서

6

M Guess what, Mom? I <u>won a prize</u> for my science project today!	**남** 있잖아요, 엄마. 전 오늘 과학 프로젝트로 상을 받았어요!
W That's great! What was <u>your project about</u> again?	**여** 대단하구나! 프로젝트가 무엇에 관한 것이었다고 했지?

M I made a model of a rocket ship. The teacher said it was the best project she'd ever seen. She even said I should design rockets.

W Wonderful! You did a good job.

남 로켓선 모형을 만들었어요. 선생님께서 보신 것 중 최고의 프로젝트라고 말씀하셨어요. 선생님께서는 심지어 제가 로켓을 디자인해야 한다고 하셨어요.

여 멋지구나! 정말 잘했다.

<table><tr><td>Vocabulary</td><td>win 상을 타다   prize 상   project 프로젝트, 계획   model 모형   rocket ship 로켓선   design 디자인하다</td></tr></table>

W Are you enjoying your soup, Sam?

M Yeah, it's delicious. I didn't know you could cook so well, Tammy.

W Well, I just used my grandmother's old recipe. I added some extra peppers, though.

M That must be why it's so spicy. Still, I think it's an excellent dish.

여 수프 맛 괜찮니, Sam?

남 응. 정말 맛있어. 난 네가 이렇게 요리를 잘하는지 몰랐어, Tammy.

여 음. 난 그냥 우리 할머니의 오래된 요리법을 이용했을 뿐이야. 하지만 후추를 조금 더 넣긴 했지.

남 그래서 수프가 많이 매운 건가 보네. 하지만 정말 훌륭한 음식이라고 생각해.

<table><tr><td>Vocabulary</td><td>recipe 요리법   add 더하다, 추가하다   extra 여분의   pepper 후추   spicy 매운   dish 음식</td></tr></table>

W Good morning, class. Today I have the results of our bake sale this past weekend. We raised over 5,000 dollars for the poor African children! Well done, everybody. Tammy's fudge brownies sold more than any other dish. Those brownies alone made over 500 dollars! Great job. All in all, it was a big success.

여 좋은 아침이에요, 여러분. 오늘 난 지난 주말에 했던 빵 바자회 행사의 결과를 가지고 있어요. 우린 가난한 아프리카 어린이들을 위해 5,000달러 이상을 모았답니다! 모두들 정말 잘했어요. Tammy의 퍼지 브라우니가 다른 어떤 것보다 더 많이 팔렸어요. 이 브라우니 만으로 500달러 이상을 벌었답니다! 아주 훌륭해요. 대체로, 빵 바자회는 대성공이었습니다.

<table><tr><td>Vocabulary</td><td>bake sale 빵 바자회(기금 마련을 위해 빵 등을 파는 행사)   raise 모으다   poor 가난한   alone 혼자
all in all 대체로   success 성공</td></tr></table>

UNIT II WILL YOU DO ME A FAVOR?

Check Up

01 a **02** 1. T 2. F

03 **A** Andrew, <u>can I ask you a favor?</u>

B Of course. <u>What is it?</u>

A I have to type a paper for history class tomorrow, but my computer just broke down. <u>Can I use your computer?</u>

B <u>Sure, you can.</u>

Check Up Scripts

01

M Hey, Ann, would you do me a favor?

W Of course. What is it?

M I forgot to mail this package this morning. Can you take it by the post office on your way out?

W Sure, I can.

남 Ann, 부탁 하나 들어 줄래?

여 물론이지. 뭔데?

남 난 오늘 아침에 이 소포를 부치는 것을 잊어 버렸어. 나가는 길에 우체국에 소포를 가져다 주겠니?

여 그럼.

Vocabulary	favor 부탁 mail 부치다 package 소포

02

W Robert, will you do me a favor?

M Sure, Jane. What is it?

W I left my wallet at home and I need to borrow 10 dollars for lunch.

M Sorry, I'm afraid I can't help you. I don't have any money now.

W Oh, what should I do?

M Why don't you ask Ted?

W Okay.

여 Robert, 부탁 하나 들어 줄래?

남 물론이지, Jane. 뭔데?

여 난 집에 지갑을 두고 와서 점심 사 먹을 돈 10달러를 빌려야 해.

남 미안하지만 도와줄 수 없구나. 난 지금 돈이 없거든.

여 아. 그럼 어쩌지?

남 Ted에게 부탁해봐.

여 알겠어.

Vocabulary	wallet 지갑

03

A Andrew, can I ask you a favor?

B Of course. What is it?

A I have to type a paper for history class tomorrow, but my computer just broke down. Can I use your computer?

B Sure, you can.

A Andrew, 부탁 하나 해도 될까?

B 물론이지. 뭔데?

A 난 내일 있을 역사 수업을 위한 과제물을 써야하는데, 내 컴퓨터가 방금 고장이 났어. 네 것을 좀 사용해도 되니?

B 그럼. 물론 괜찮지.

Vocabulary	type 타자 치다 paper 과제물 history 역사 break down 고장 나다

1

M Excuse me, ma'am? Could you help me?

W Of course. What is it?

M I'm looking for the bank, but I don't know this area very well. Do you know where it is?

W Yeah. Go straight on Jackson Street until you reach the coffee shop. Then turn left. The bank is the third building on your right.

M Thanks.

남	실례합니다. 부인. 저를 도와주시겠어요?
여	물론이죠. 무슨 일이세요?
남	전 은행을 찾고 있는데, 이 지역을 잘 모릅니다. 은행이 어딘지 아시나요?
여	네. Jackson Street에서 커피숍에 이를 때까지 직진하세요. 그런 다음 왼쪽으로 도세요. 은행은 당신의 오른쪽에서 세 번째 건물이에요.
남	감사합니다.

> **Vocabulary**   look for ~을 찾다   area 지역   straight 똑바로   until ~할 때까지   reach 이르다. 닿다

2

M Annette, I need to study hard for my math test, but I'm not good at math. Can you help me?

W Sorry, I'm afraid I can't. I'm meeting my friends at the mall tonight.

M Aw, but that test is tomorrow!

W Well, I'm sorry, but I've already made plans tonight.

M Oh, what should I do then? My mom will be very upset if I fail the test again.

남	Annette, 난 수학 시험을 위해 열심히 공부해야 하는데, 수학을 잘 하지 못해. 날 좀 도와 줄래?
여	미안하지만 안돼. 난 오늘 밤에 쇼 핑몰에서 친구들을 만나거든.
남	아, 하지만 시험이 내일이야!
여	음, 미안하지만 오늘밤에는 이미 계획이 있어서.
남	아, 난 그럼 어떻게 해야 하지? 내가 만약 또 시험에 낙제하면 우리 엄마는 아주 화를 내실 텐데.

> **Vocabulary**   math 수학   be good at ~을 잘하다   already 이미   plan 계획   upset 화가 난   fail 낙제하다, 실패하다

3

[The answering machine beeps.]

M Hey, Linda, it's John. Will you do me a favor? My family and I are going on vacation next week. Could you get our mail and water our plants while we're away? And you know that we have a puppy. Since we can't take him, I hope you can feed and walk him every day. If you can do it, call me back. Talk to you later!

[자동응답기 소리]

남 안녕. Linda. 난 John이야. 부탁 하나 들어줄래? 우리 가족과 난 다음 주에 휴가를 갈 예정이야. 우리가 없는 동안 우편물을 받아 주고 식물에 물을 좀 줄 수 있겠니? 그리고 우리에게 강아지가 있다는 것 알지. 강아지를 데리고 갈 수 없기 때문에 난 네가 매일 강아지 먹이를 주고 산책을 시켜 줬으면 좋겠어. 만약에 할 수 있으면 다시 전화를 줘. 나중에 얘기하자!

> **Vocabulary**   go on a vacation 휴가를 가다   mail 우편물   water 물을 주다   plant 식물   since ~이기 때문에   feed 먹이를 주다   walk 산책 시키다

4

W Marvin, would you help me with something?

M What do you need?

W Well, my television is not working. Could you look at it?

M I can only fix DVD players. But my friend Bob knows a lot about TVs. Why don't you give him a call? Here's his phone number.

W Thanks!

여 Marvin, 날 좀 도와 줄래?

남 뭐가 필요한데?

여 음. 텔레비전이 작동하지 않아. 좀 봐 줄 수 있니?

남 난 DVD 플레이어만 고칠 수 있어. 하지만 내 친구 Bob이 TV에 대해 많이 알지. 그에게 전화를 해 보는 게 어때? 여기 그 애 전화번호야.

여 고마워!

Vocabulary	work 작동하다 give a call 전화하다

5

① W I can't find any boxes here.

M Oh, I put the boxes in my room.

② W Oh, these boxes are too heavy. Will you please help me?

M Sure. Give some of them to me.

③ W Do you know where my textbook is?

M I have no idea. Why don't you look in your drawer?

④ W Hey, what's the matter? You look tired.

M I had a very tough day at school today.

⑤ W It's too hot outside. I think we should just stay home.

M That's a better idea.

① 여 난 여기서 상자를 찾을 수 없어.

남 아. 내가 내 방에 두었어.

② 여 아. 이 상자들은 너무 무거워. 나 좀 도와 줄래?

남 물론이지. 내게 좀 건네 줘.

③ 여 넌 내 교과서가 어디 있는지 아니?

남 모르겠는데. 서랍을 한번 봐.

④ 여 얘, 무슨 일이니? 피곤해 보인다.

남 오늘 학교에서 너무 힘들었어.

⑤ 여 밖은 너무 더워. 난 우리가 그냥 집에 있어야 한다고 생각해.

남 그게 더 나은 생각이구나.

Vocabulary	heavy 무거운 textbook 교과서 drawer 서랍 tough 힘든 stay 머물다

6

W It has been almost three months, but half of our city is still in ruins. Many people lost their homes and lives during the powerful earthquake. And many people need help now. Millions in the city are still without electricity and water. It is said that it will take many years to repair all the damage.

여 거의 세 달 정도가 지났지만 우리의 도시 절반 정도가 아직 폐허입니다. 많은 사람들은 강력한 지진 동안 집과 생명을 잃었습니다. 그리고 많은 사람들은 지금 도움이 필요합니다. 도시의 수백만 명이 여전히 전기와 물이 없이 살고 있습니다. 이 모든 피해를 복구하는 데는 수 년의 세월이 걸릴 것이라고 합니다.

Vocabulary	during ~동안 powerful 강력한 earthquake 지진 million 백 만 electricity 전기 damage 피해

7

W Hey, Jack, can you <u>do</u> <u>me</u> <u>a favor</u>?	**여** 안녕, Jack. 내 부탁 좀 들어 줄래?
M Sure. What is it?	**남** 물론이지. 뭔데?
W My car is <u>in the repair</u> shop, and I need a ride to the Park Office Building after work. <u>Could you drive me</u>?	**여** 내 차가 지금 수리점에 있는데, 퇴근 후에 Park Office 건물까지 차편이 필요해. 나 좀 태워 줄래?
M Sure. I'll go to your office by 7 p.m. <u>Is that</u> OK?	**남** 물론이지. 네 사무실에 오후 7시까지 갈게. 괜찮니?
W Yeah, <u>thanks a lot</u>.	**여** 응, 정말 고마워.

> **Vocabulary**　repair shop 수리점

8

W Could you do me a favor, Robbie?	**여** 부탁 하나 들어 줄래, Robbie?
M Of course. <u>What do you</u> need?	**남** 물론이지. 뭐가 필요하니?
W I need help preparing a special cake for Cindy's party. <u>She's leaving town</u> for her new school, so we're having a party for her on Friday.	**여** 난 Cindy의 파티를 위한 특별한 케이크를 준비하는 데 도움이 필요해. 그 앤 새 학교 때문에 마을을 떠날 거야. 그래서 우린 금요일에 그녀를 위해 파티를 할 거야.
M <u>When are you making</u> the cake?	**남** 언제 케이크를 만드는데?
W The day before the party.	**여** 파티 전날에.
M Oh, sorry, I have to <u>visit my</u> grandmother on that day.	**남** 아, 미안하지만 그날 우리 할머니를 찾아뵈어야 해.
W Oh, I heard that your grandmother is <u>in the hospital</u> now. I hope <u>she'll get better soon</u>.	**여** 아, 너희 할머니께서 지금 입원 중이시라고 들었어. 할머니께서 얼른 건강해지시길 빌게.
M Thanks.	**남** 고마워.

> **Vocabulary**　prepare 준비하다　in the hospital 입원 중인　get better (병 따위가) 나아지다

UNIT III ARE YOU SURE?

Check Up

01 a **02** wash his father's car, play basketball

03 A We've been waiting for nearly 20 minutes. <u>Do you think we'll be seated soon?</u>

  B Don't worry. We'll be seated soon.

  A <u>Are you sure?</u>

  B Yeah, <u>I'm pretty sure</u> it will be just a few more minutes.

  A I hope so. I'm really hungry.

Check Up Scripts

01

W Chris, why did you want to see me?

M Oh, Jane. I have a question.

W What is it?

M Are you sure that Rose will come to the party tomorrow night?

W Yes. She said she would come.

M Oh, I can't wait to see her. I haven't seen her since last month.

여 Chris, 왜 날 보자고 했니?

남 아, Jane. 질문이 있어서.

여 뭔데?

남 Rose가 내일 밤 파티에 오는 거 확실하니?

여 응. 올 거라고 말했어.

남 난 그녀를 볼 것이 너무 기대가 돼. 지난 달 이후로 못 만났거든.

Vocabulary	since ~이래로

02

W Hey, Bill. Do you think you can play basketball with us on Saturday?

M Uh, that depends. What time are you guys playing?

W At about 3:00 that afternoon. Do you have other plans?

M No, I'm sure I can play. I have to wash my father's car first that afternoon, but that won't take long.

여 안녕, Bill. 너 토요일에 우리와 함께 농구할 수 있을 것 같니?

남 어, 상황에 따라 달라. 너희들은 몇 시에 농구 할 거야?

여 그 날 오후 3시쯤에. 다른 계획이 있니?

남 아냐, 난 확실히 할 수 있어. 그 날 오후에 아버지의 자동차 세차를 먼저 해야 하지만, 시간이 그리 오래 걸리지는 않을 거야.

Vocabulary	depend ~에 달려 있다	take (시간이) ~걸리다

03

A We've been waiting for nearly 20 minutes. Do you think we'll be seated soon?

B Don't worry. We'll be seated soon.

A Are you sure?

B Yeah, I'm pretty sure it will be just a few

A 우린 거의 20분 정도나 기다리고 있어. 우리가 곧 자리에 앉을 수 있을 거라고 생각하니?

B 걱정하지마. 우린 곧 앉게 될 거야.

A 확실해?

B 응. 난 몇 분만 더 기다리면 될 거라고 확신해.

more minutes.

A I hope so. I'm really hungry.

A 그러길 바래. 난 너무 배가 고파.

Actual Test   1 ②   2 ④   3 ⑤   4 ③   5 ①   6 ④   7 ⑤   8 ② | p.20

M Can you help me, ma'am?

W Sure. What is it?

M Someone stole my bike from school.

W I see. Are you sure it was stolen?

M Yes, I'm sure. I always park in the same place. Do you think you will catch the thief?

W I'm not sure about that, but I'll try to.

남   저 좀 도와주실 수 있으세요?

여   물론이지. 뭔데?

남   누군가 학교에서 제 자전거를 훔쳐 갔어요.

여   그렇구나. 도둑 맞은 것이 확실하니?

남   네, 확실해요. 전 항상 같은 곳에 자전거를 두거든요. 도둑을 잡을 수 있을까요?

여   확실하진 않지만, 노력해 보마.

Vocabulary   steal 훔치다   park 주차하다   same 똑 같은   place 장소   catch 잡다   thief 도둑

2

M Hey, today is Kevin's birthday, right?

W No. His birthday is a week from today.

M Are you sure? I thought his birthday is June 22nd.

W I'm sure. I asked him yesterday.

남   얘, 오늘이 Kevin의 생일 맞지?

여   아니야. 그의 생일은 오늘로부터 일주일 후야.

남   확실하니? 난 그의 생일이 6월 22일이라고 생각했는데.

여   확실해. 어제 물어봤거든.

Vocabulary   birthday 생일   June 6월

W Did you enjoy everything, sir?

M Yes, everything was wonderful. I especially liked the potatoes.

W Excellent. Are you sure that you wouldn't like some dessert? We serve great ice cream.

M Yes, I'm sure. I'm full. I appreciate it, though.

W I'll get your bill, then.

M Thank you.

여   (음식은) 전부 괜찮으셨습니까, 손님?

남   네, 모든 것이 훌륭했어요. 전 특히 감자가 맛있었어요.

여   다행이군요. 후식은 드시지 않으시겠어요? 저희는 아주 맛있는 아이스크림을 제공하고 있습니다.

남   네, 괜찮아요. 전 배가 불러요. 어쨌든 고마워요.

여   그러시다면 계산서를 가져다 드리겠습니다.

남   감사합니다.

Vocabulary   especially 특히   dessert 후식   serve 제공하다   full 배가 부른   bill 계산서

M Hey, Janice, how was your weekend?

W It was nice. I drove up to Boston to visit my mother.

M How's she doing?

W Okay. She said that my sister just got a new job in New York. She'll move to New York next month.

M Great! She must be excited.

W Yeah, but she's also sad because she doesn't want to leave Buffalo. She really loves her life there.

M I see. I'm sure that she will love the city.

Question Where does Janice's sister live now?

남 얘, Janice. 주말은 어떻게 보냈니?

여 즐거웠어. 난 엄마를 방문하기 위해 Boston까지 운전했어.

남 어머니는 어떠셔?

여 잘 지내셔. 엄마가 말씀하시길, 최근에 우리 언니가 New York에 새 직장을 얻었대. 언니는 다음 달에 New York으로 이사 갈 거야.

남 잘됐구나! 그녀는 아주 흥분해 있겠구나.

여 응, 하지만 Buffalo를 떠나기 싫어해서 슬퍼하고 있어. 그녀는 그 곳에서의 삶을 정말 좋아하거든.

남 그렇구나. 그녀가 그 도시를 좋아할 거라고 확신해.

질문 Janice의 언니는 현재 어디 살고 있는가?

Vocabulary	move 이사 가다 excited 흥분한

W Playing this instrument helps me relax. I love learning new songs by Mozart. I also love playing songs for my friends. The black and white keys exercise my fingers and my mind. I'm sure I will become a great player one day.

여 이 악기를 연주하는 것은 내가 편안해지도록 도와 줍니다. 나는 모차르트가 쓴 새로운 노래들을 배우는 것을 좋아합니다. 나는 친구들을 위해 노래를 연주하는 것도 좋아합니다. 검고 하얀 선반은 내 손가락과 마음을 단련시킵니다. 나는 언젠가 위대한 연주가가 될 것이라고 확신합니다.

Vocabulary	instrument 악기 relax 편안해지다 exercise 연습시키다 mind 마음 become ～이 되다

M Hey, have you made out the schedule for this weekend, yet?

W Yeah. Louis and Ryan are both working for eight hours on Friday: from 12 p.m. to 8 p.m.

M Great. What about Saturday?

W Louis, Ryan, and Nick are all working that day. Do you think that's enough people?

M I'm sure that will be fine.

W Oh, and Nick is coming in for four hours on Sunday: from 2 p.m. to 6 p.m. He'll be by himself.

M That's fine.

남 이번 주말을 위한 일정은 다 작성했나요?

여 네. Louis와 Ryan 두 사람이 금요일 오후12시부터 8시까지 함께 일할 겁니다.

남 좋군요. 토요일은 어떤가요?

여 Louis, Ryan, Nick이 그 날 모두 일을 할 겁니다. 충분한 인원이라고 생각하세요?

남 괜찮을 거라고 확신해요.

여 아, 그리고 Nick은 일요일에 와서 오후 2시부터 6시까지 네 시간 동안 일을 할 겁니다. 그는 혼자 일할 거예요.

남 좋습니다.

7 

W Jason, <u>have</u> <u>you</u> <u>heard</u> from Liz?

M Yes, Ms. Dalton. I know <u>she's</u> <u>really</u> <u>sick</u>.

W So your partner for your class project <u>can't</u> <u>help</u> <u>you</u>. Do you think that <u>you'll</u> <u>finish</u> <u>on</u> <u>time</u>?

M Yeah, <u>I</u> <u>think</u> <u>so</u>. We're almost done. I can finish <u>the</u> <u>rest</u> <u>of</u> <u>it</u> by myself.

여　Jason, Liz로부터 소식 들었니?

남　네, Dalton 선생님. 전 그 애가 많이 아프다는 것을 알아요.

여　그럼 학급 프로젝트를 함께 할 네 파트너는 널 도와줄 수 없겠구나. 네가 시간에 맞추어 끝낼 수 있다고 생각하니?

남　네, 그럴 것 같아요. 저희는 거의 완성했거든요. 나머지 부분은 저 혼자 끝낼 수 있어요.

8 

W Well, <u>the</u> <u>new</u> <u>school</u> <u>year</u> begins in a few days.

M I know. There are going to be <u>at</u> <u>least</u> <u>200</u> <u>more</u> <u>students</u> in my grade this year.

W Whoa! That's a lot.

M I know. I think we should <u>build</u> <u>another</u> <u>school</u> for these new students.

W Are you sure <u>that's</u> <u>a</u> <u>good</u> <u>idea</u>? That would cost <u>a</u> <u>lot</u> <u>of</u> <u>money</u>.

M Well, we have to do something. There are <u>too</u> <u>many</u> <u>students</u> in our school.

여　음, 며칠 있으면 새 학년이 시작되는군요.

남　맞아요. 올해 제가 맡는 학년의 학생 수는 적어도 200명 이상이 될 거에요.

여　우와. 아주 많네요.

남　그러게요. 전 우리가 이 새로운 학생들을 위해 또 하나의 학교 시설을 지어야 한다고 생각해요.

여　그게 좋은 생각이라고 확신하세요? 그러면 비용이 많이 들 거에요.

남　음, 우린 무언가를 해야만 해요. 우리 학교에는 학생들이 너무 많아요.

UNIT IV TAKE IT EASY!

01 c   **02** b

03 **A** Good morning, Linda. How are you?

    B I'm really upset.

    A Why are you so upset?

    B Because my brother broke my glasses.

    A Hey, calm down.

Check Up Scripts

01

W Good morning, Mr. Barns. How are you feeling today?

M Not well. My arm hurts. I think I hurt it yesterday.

W Oh? Did you have an accident?

M I did fall on it, but it didn't hurt until this morning. Could you look at it?

W Sure. Hmm. It doesn't look broken.

여 좋은 아침입니다, Barns씨. 오늘 기분이 어떠세요?

남 별로 좋지 않아요. 팔에 통증이 있어요. 전 어제 다친 것 같아요.

여 아니? 사고를 당했나요?

남 넘어졌는데, 오늘 아침까지는 아프지 않았어요. 좀 봐주시겠어요?

여 물론이죠. 흠. 골절이 된 것 같지는 않네요.

Vocabulary	hurt 아프다 have an accident 사고를 당하다 fall 넘어지다

02

M Excuse me, Ms. Sharp. Can I talk to you now?

W Sure, Kevin. What is it?

M I just don't understand this math problem.

W Take it easy. It's really very simple. Look at the example on page 52.

M Let's see. Oh, I think I understand it now. Thank you!

남 실례합니다. Sharp 선생님. 지금 말씀을 좀 드릴 수 있을까요?

여 물론이지. Kevin. 무엇 때문이니?

남 전 이 수학 문제가 이해가 안돼요.

여 진정해. 그 문제는 정말 간단하단다. 52페이지의 예를 보렴.

남 볼게요. 아, 이제 이해가 되는 것 같아요. 감사해요!

Vocabulary	understand 이해하다 simple 간단한

03

A Good morning, Linda. How are you?

B I'm really upset.

A Why are you so upset?

B Because my brother broke my glasses.

A Hey, calm down.

A 안녕, Linda. 오늘 기분이 어떠니?

B 난 정말 화가 났어.

A 왜 그렇게 화가 났니?

B 왜냐하면 내 남동생이 안경을 깨뜨렸거든.

A 이봐, 진정해.

Vocabulary	upset 화가 난 break 깨뜨리다 glasses 안경

Actual Test

1 ①　**2** ②　**3** ④　**4** ④　**5** ⑤　**6** ②　**7** ①　**8** ③　　| p.26

1

W Excuse me! Can you please help me?

M Yes, ma'am. Is something wrong?

W I think I lost my suitcase! We just landed and it's not here! Even my passport was in there!

M All right, just calm down.

W But that suitcase had everything in it! My laptop computer, my wallet, and my clothes.

M All right. I'll get someone to help you right away.

여 실례합니다. 저 좀 도와주실래요?

남 네, 부인. 뭐가 잘못되었나요?

여 제가 여행 가방을 잃어버린 것 같아요. 저희는 방금 내렸는데, 가방이 여기 없어요! 심지어 제 여권도 거기 있어요!

남 그렇군요. 진정하십시오.

여 하지만 그 여행 가방에는 모든 것이 들어 있단 말이에요! 제 노트북과, 지갑, 옷들이요.

남 알겠습니다. 당장 사람을 시켜 당신을 도와드리도록 하겠습니다.

Vocabulary	suitcase 여행 가방　　land 착륙하다　　laptop 휴대용 컴퓨터　　passport 여권　　right away 당장

2

W Jeremy, you look worried. What's wrong?

M My sister had a car accident last weekend. She hurt her neck.

W Oh, I'm sorry to hear that. Is she OK?

M Yeah, she's getting better, but I'm still worried about her.

여 Jeremy, 넌 걱정스러워 보이네. 무슨 문제가 있니?

남 내 여동생이 지난 주말에 교통 사고를 당했어. 그녀는 목을 다쳤어.

여 안됐구나. 그녀는 괜찮니?

남 응. 그 앤 점점 낫고 있어. 하지만 난 여전히 걱정이 돼.

Vocabulary	worried 걱정스러운　　have a car accident 교통사고를 당하다

3

M How are you today, Dr. Smith?

W I'm doing fine. It's been very busy, though.

M By the way, Melissa Hart called. She set up an appointment for Thursday at 10 a.m.

W I see. What does she need?

M She says it's her heart medicine. She needs more of it.

W Okay. Did she leave her number?

M Yes. It's 555-6799.

W Okay. Thanks for the message.

남 오늘 기분이 어때요, Smith 선생님?

여 전 괜찮아요. 하지만 정말 바쁘군요.

남 그런데 Melissa Hart씨가 전화했어요. 그녀는 목요일 오전 10시에 약속을 잡았어요.

여 그렇군요. 무엇이 필요한 거죠?

남 심장약 때문에요. 심장약이 더 필요합니다.

여 알겠어요. 그녀는 전화번호를 남겼나요?

남 네. 555-6799번입니다.

여 알았어요. 메시지 고마워요.

Vocabulary	set up an appointment 약속을 정하다　　heart 심장　　medicine 약　　leave 남기다

M Hey, Tammy. How are you today?

W Well, I'm a little nervous, Mr. Potter. Today's my first day of this school.

M Ah, I know how that feels.

W Really?

M Yeah, I remember my first day at this school 20 years ago. I was just a nervous 13-year-old kid entering a large, new school. But don't worry! You'll get along well with everyone.

남 얘. Tammy. 넌 오늘 기분이 어떠니?

여 음, 전 조금 긴장이 되요, Potter 선생님. 오늘이 이 학교에서의 첫 날이거든요.

남 아. 난 그게 어떤 기분인지 알지.

여 정말이요?

남 그렇단다. 난 20년 전 이 학교에서의 첫 날을 기억하지. 난 크고 새로운 학교에 들어가며 떨고 있던 13살짜리 소년이었지. 하지만 걱정하지 마! 넌 모두와 잘 지내게 될 거야.

Vocabulary	ago ~전에 enter 들어가다 get along with ~와 잘 지내다

[The answering machine beeps.]

M Hello, Barry. This is Jim. I heard your brother's company is closing down. I'm sorry to hear that. I know that it is hard to find work now. In fact, I think that my uncle's company will have some new jobs available soon. If your brother is interested, please let me know. Bye.

[자동응답기 소리]

남 안녕. Barry. 난 Jim이야. 너희 형의 회사가 문을 닫는다고 들었어. 유감이야. 난 요새 일을 구하기가 어렵다는 것을 알아. 사실은 우리 삼촌 회사에서 곧 새로운 일자리가 생길 것 같아. 만약 네 형이 관심이 있다면 알려줘. 안녕.

Vocabulary	close down 폐쇄하다 in fact 사실 available 이용 가능한 interested 관심이 있는

① **M** How do you feel today?

  W I feel awful.

② **M** Are you feeling OK?

  W Well, I hope you get better.

③ **M** I didn't pass the science test.

  W Oh, that's too bad.

④ **M** Oh, I think we'll miss our plane.

  W Calm down. It will be okay.

⑤ **M** My grandfather is very sick.

  W I'm sorry to hear that.

① **남** 오늘 기분이 어떠니?

  여 난 기분이 아주 안 좋아.

② **남** 오늘 기분 괜찮아?

  여 음, 난 네가 빨리 낫길 바라.

③ **남** 난 과학 시험을 통과하지 못했어.

  여 안됐구나.

④ **남** 아. 난 우리가 비행기를 놓칠 것 같아.

  여 진정해. 괜찮을 거야.

⑤ **남** 우리 할아버지께서 많이 편찮으셔.

  여 유감이야.

Vocabulary	awful 끔찍한 pass 통과하다 miss 놓치다

W Are you <u>planning</u> <u>a</u> <u>trip</u> out of town? Then plan your stay at the Swan Hotel. You can <u>take</u> <u>it</u> <u>easy</u> and enjoy beautiful views here. And our hotels are famous <u>for</u> <u>the</u> <u>largest</u> <u>rooms</u> and greatest service around. We also have five-star restaurants, and you'll love <u>our</u> <u>delicious</u> <u>food</u>. So what are you waiting for? <u>Make</u> <u>a</u> <u>reservation</u> today!

여　교외로 여행을 떠날 계획이신가요? 그렇다면 Swan 호텔에 머무를 계획을 세우세요. 이 곳에서 당신은 휴식을 취하고 아름다운 경치를 즐기실 수 있습니다. 그리고 저희 호텔은 가장 넓은 객실과 훌륭한 서비스로 유명합니다. 저희 는 최고 등급의 레스토랑을 소유하고 있으며, 당신은 맛있는 음식에 만족하실 겁니다. 무엇을 망설이세요? 오늘 예약 하 십시오!

Vocabulary	plan 계획하다　trip 여행　view 경치　be famous for ~으로 유명하다　five-star 별 다섯 개의, 최고 등급의
	wait for ~을 기다리다　make a reservation 예약을 하다

W Ted, <u>you</u> <u>look</u> <u>terrible</u>. What's wrong?

M Oh, <u>I'm</u> <u>really</u> <u>upset</u>. I hate my reading club!

W Why? I thought <u>you</u> <u>liked</u> <u>your</u> club.

M Not at all. There's just <u>too</u> <u>much</u> <u>work</u> to do. <u>It's</u> <u>driving</u> <u>me</u> crazy!

여　Ted, 넌 정말 기분이 안 좋아 보여. 무슨 일이니?

남　아, 난 정말 화가 나. 난 독서 클럽이 너무 싫어!

여　왜? 난 네가 그 동아리를 좋아하고 있다고 생각했는데.

남　전혀 그렇지 않아. 할 일이 너무 많거든. 그건 날 미치게 만들어!

Vocabulary	terrible 끔찍한　drive someone crazy ~을 미치게 하다

UNIT V HELP YOURSELF.

🌀 Check Up

01 b, c **02** b

03 A <u>Do you want some more pizza?</u>
B Thanks, but <u>I'm full.</u>
A <u>Would you like</u> some more soda then?
B <u>Yes, please.</u>
A Here you are.

Check Up Scripts

01

W Oh, dear? We need to get some fruit from the store.

M Okay. Let's get some apples, then. The kids love those.

W Sure. Do you want to get some grapes, too?

M I don't think we'll eat them quickly enough. Those spoil quickly. Let's get some bananas, instead. I need some for my cereal.

여 여보. 우린 가게에서 과일을 좀 사야 해요.

남 그래요. 그럼 사과를 좀 삽시다. 아이들이 좋아하잖아요.

여 그래요. 포도도 살까요?

남 포도는 충분히 빨리 먹지 못할 것 같아요. 포도는 쉽게 상하잖아요. 대신 바나나를 삽시다. 시리얼을 위해 좀 필요해요.

Vocabulary	quickly 빨리 enough 충분히 spoil 상하다 cereal 시리얼

02

M Hey, Sarah. Do you know what time it is?

W Let's see. It's almost one.

M Our lunch hour's almost up. We need to head back to the class.

W Mr. Lynch won't mind if we're a little late.

M Maybe, but I have a lot of homework to do.

남 이봐. Sarah. 너 지금 몇 시인지 아니?

여 어디 보자. 거의 한 시가 다 되었어.

남 점심시간이 거의 끝났구나. 교실로 돌아가야겠어.

여 Lynch 선생님께선 우리가 조금 늦어도 신경 쓰시지 않을 거야.

남 아마도. 하지만 난 숙제가 많거든.

Vocabulary	head back 돌아가다 mind 신경 쓰다

03

A Do you want some more pizza?

B Thanks, but I'm full.

A Would you like some more soda then?

B Yes, please.

A Here you are.

A 피자를 더 드실래요?

B 고맙지만 배가 불러요.

A 그럼 음료수를 더 마시겠어요?

B 그래요.

A 여기 있어요.

Vocabulary	full 배가 부른

Actual Test
1 ④   2 ②   3 ①   4 ⑤   5 ③   6 ③   7 ②   8 ①
| p.32

W ① He is drinking milk.
② She is preparing some food.
③ He is buying some groceries.
④ They are baking cookies.
⑤ She cut her finger with the knife.

여 ① 그는 우유를 마시고 있다.
② 그녀는 음식을 준비 중이다.
③ 그는 식료품을 사고 있다.
④ 그들은 쿠키를 굽고 있다.
⑤ 그녀는 칼에 손을 베었다.

Vocabulary	grocery 식료품 bake 굽다

W Come on, Timmy. You haven't eaten any vegetables.
M No, that's okay. I'm full, Mom.
W But vegetables are good for you. You need to eat some.
M Oh, Mom. You know I never eat vegetables. I don't like the way they taste.
W Oh, Timmy. I'm so worried about you.

여 제발. Timmy. 넌 채소를 계속 먹지 않고 있잖니.
남 싫어요. 됐어요. 전 배 불러요. 엄마.
여 하지만 채소는 네 몸에 좋아. 넌 채소를 좀 먹어야 해.
남 오, 엄마. 제가 채소를 안 먹는 걸 아시잖아요. 난 채소가 너무 맛이 없어요.
여 오, Timmy. 난 네가 정말 걱정되는구나.

Vocabulary	vegetable 채소 taste ～한 맛이 나다

M Do you want a tasty snack? Then try East Seas Ramen Noodles! There are over 12 delicious flavors of noodles. They cost less than a bag of potato chips or crackers, too. All you have to do is add water, boil, and enjoy! You can pick them up in any grocery or convenience store, too. So help yourself to East Seas Ramen Noodles today!

남 맛있는 음식을 원하세요? 그렇다면 East Seas Ramen Noodles를 먹어보세요! 맛있는 라면의 맛이 12가지 이상 있답니다. 그리고 라면의 가격은 감자칩이나 크래커보다 더 싸지요. 당신은 물을 넣어 끓이고 즐기기만 하면 됩니다! 식품점이나 편의점 어디에서나 고르실 수 있어요. 그러니 오늘 East Seas Ramen Noodles를 마음껏 드셔보세요!

Vocabulary	tasty 맛있는 snack 간단한 식사 flavor 맛, 풍미 less 더 적게 boil 끓이다 pick up 집어 들다 convenience store 편의점

4

W This is excellent coffee. Can I have some more, please?
M Certainly. Help yourself.
W Also, do you sell a coffee mug like this? I'd like to add it to my collection.

여 이거 정말 맛있는 커피군요. 좀 더 주실래요?
남 물론이죠. 마음껏 드세요.
여 그리고 이것과 같은 머그컵도 파시나요? 난 이것을 내 수집품에 추가하고 싶어요.

M You have a very special hobby. I think we have several kinds of mugs in the gift shop.

W Oh, I would like to see the mugs you sell.

M Sure. Come this way.

남 아주 특별한 취미를 가지셨군요. 선물 가게에 몇 가지 종류의 머그컵이 있을 거에요.

여 아, 당신이 파는 머그컵을 보고 싶군요.

남 그래요. 이쪽으로 오세요.

5

W Good day, sir. Would you like to try one of our fish plates?

M I think I would, please. Can I have the fish with rice plate, please?

W Sure. You can also order one other item with that dish.

M Hmm. I'd like some salad with that, please.

W All right. Will there be anything else, sir?

M That will be all, thank you.

여 기분 좋은 날입니다. 저희의 생선 요리를 드셔 보시겠어요?

남 네, 그러죠. 밥과 함께 생선 요리를 주시겠어요?

여 알겠습니다. 그리고 음식과 함께 다른 요리를 하나 더 주문하실 수 있습니다.

남 음. 전 샐러드를 먹겠어요.

여 알겠습니다. 다른 필요하신 건 없으세요?

남 그게 다에요. 감사합니다.

6

W Would you like some dessert?

M Yes, I'd like to have chocolate cake. It says here that it's 50 % off now. Is that right?

W Yes, sir. It's only 3 dollars now.

M Oh, great. I'll have it.

여 디저트를 드시겠어요?

남 네, 전 초콜릿 케이크를 먹고 싶군요. 여기 50% 할인된다고 나와있는데, 맞나요?

여 네, 그렇습니다. 3달러 밖에 하지 않습니다.

남 오, 잘됐군요. 그걸 먹겠어요.

7

M It's so good to see you again, Aunt Ruth.

W It's good to see you again, Ryan. Do you want some more stew?

M No, thanks, I'm full. Say, did you paint your kitchen?

W Yes. We decided to try a new color.

M It looks really nice.

W Thank you. I painted it myself. I also got a bigger table.

M I see that. Did you sell your old table?

남 다시 뵙게 되어 좋아요. Ruth 이모.

여 나도 다시 봐서 좋구나. Ryan. 스튜를 좀 더 먹겠니?

남 감사하지만, 배가 불러요. 음, 부엌에 페인트를 칠하셨어요?

여 그렇단다. 우린 새로운 색깔을 시도해 보기로 결정했거든.

남 정말 보기 좋군요.

여 고맙구나. 내가 직접 페인트를 칠했지. 난 더 큰 탁자도 마련했단다.

남 그렇네요. 원래 있던 탁자는 파셨나요?

W No. It's in our bedroom.

여 아니. 침실에 있어.

Vocabulary   paint 페인트를 칠하다   decide to ~하기로 결정하다

8

W Would you like <u>another</u> <u>hot</u> <u>dog</u>, Eddie?

여 핫도그를 하나 더 먹을래. Eddie?

M Yes, please. <u>These</u> <u>taste</u> <u>really</u> <u>good</u>, Wendy.

남 응. 먹을게. 이것들은 정말 맛이 좋구나. Wendy.

W Thanks. I think <u>you</u> <u>should</u> <u>come</u> to my neighborhood cookout then. I'll cook <u>a lot</u> <u>of things</u> on the grill.

여 고마워. 나는 네가 우리 이웃들이 모이는 야외파티에 오면 어떨까 생각되네. 그릴에 많은 음식을 구울 거야.

M That sounds great. <u>When</u> <u>is</u> <u>the</u> <u>cookout</u>?

남 멋진데. 파티가 언제야?

Vocabulary   another 또 다른   taste ~한 맛이 나다   neighborhood 이웃   cookout 야외에서 요리해 먹는 식사, 파티
grill 그릴, 석쇠

UNIT VI GO STRAIGHT TWO BLOCKS.

Check Up

p.37

01 b **02** **a.** hotel **b.** zoo **c.** bank

03 **A** Oh, excuse me. <u>Do you know where the supermarket is?</u>

B Uh, sure. <u>Go down this street</u> until you reach the bakery.

A Yes. And then?

B Turn right at the bakery and go down two more blocks. It is <u>next to the gas station</u>. <u>You can't miss it.</u>

Check Up Scripts

01

M Excuse me. Where's the bookstore?

W Go straight and when you see the 'No Parking' sign, make a left turn. It will be on your right.

M Thanks.

W No problem.

남 실례합니다. 서점이 어디죠?

여 '주차금지' 표지판이 나올 때까지 직진하셔서 왼쪽으로 도세요. 서점은 오른쪽에 있을 겁니다.

남 감사합니다.

여 천만에요.

Vocabulary	No parking 주차 금지

02

W Excuse me. Does this bus go to the zoo?

M Yeah. It's a twenty minute ride to the zoo. First we have to stop at the hotel, then we go to the zoo. Last stop is the bank.

W That sounds fine. How much is the fare?

M Actually, between 9 to 5 on weekdays, there's no fare.

여 실례합니다. 이 버스가 동물원에 가나요?

남 네. 동물원까지 20분 걸립니다. 우선 호텔에서 선 뒤 동물원에 갑니다. 마지막 역은 은행입니다.

여 좋군요. 버스 요금은 얼마죠?

남 사실 평일 9시부터 5시까지 요금은 무료입니다.

Vocabulary	fare 요금 actually 사실 between ~사이에

03

A Oh, excuse me. Do you know where the supermarket is?

B Uh, sure. Go down this street until you reach the bakery.

A Yes. And then?

B Turn right at the bakery and go down two more blocks. It is next to the gas station. <u>You can't miss it.</u>

A 실례합니다. 슈퍼마켓이 어딘지 아시나요?

B 아, 물론이죠. 빵집이 나올 때까지 이 길을 쭉 가세요.

A 네, 그 다음엔요?

B 빵집에서 오른쪽으로 돌아서 두 블록을 더 가세요. 슈퍼마켓은 주유소 옆에 있어요. 찾기 쉬우실 거예요.

Vocabulary	until ~때 까지 reach 이르다

Actual Test   1 ③ 2 ④ 3 ⑤ 4 ① 5 ① 6 ② 7 ⑤ 8 ④ | p.38

1

M Hey, Lisa, is there a park near here?

W Sure. Go up the street five blocks. It's on the other side of the Radio Station.

M Just five blocks? I don't have to drive up there, then.

W Yeah, you can just take your bike up there.

M That's exactly what I wanted to do.

| Vocabulary | exactly 정확히 |

남 얘, Lisa, 여기 근처에 공원이 있니?

여 그럼. 이 거리를 따라 다섯 블록을 가. 공원은 Radio Station의 반대편에 있어.

남 다섯 블록이라고? 그럼 운전해 갈 필요가 없겠구나.

여 응, 자전거를 타고 가면 돼.

남 바로 내가 하고 싶었던 바야.

2

M Sorry, but could you help me?

W Of course. What is it?

M I forgot to bring my cell phone and have to make a call. Is there a public phone anywhere around here?

W There's one at the front desk in the main lobby. It's right across from the bathrooms.

M Oh, right! That's where guests sign in, too, right?

W Exactly.

| Vocabulary | bring 가져 오다   make a call 전화하다   public 공중의   across from ~맞은 편에
sign in 입실/퇴실 시 서명하다 |

남 죄송하지만, 저 좀 도와주시겠어요?

여 물론이죠. 무엇 때문에 그러세요?

남 전 휴대폰을 가지고 오는 것을 잊어버렸는데 전화를 해야 해요. 이 곳에 공중 전화가 있나요?

여 메인 로비에 가시면 안내데스크에 하나 있어요. 화장실 바로 맞은 편이에요.

남 오, 그렇군요! 손님들이 서명하는 곳이죠, 맞죠?

여 맞아요.

3

M Hey, honey, do you know where the restrooms are? I spilled some soda on my shirt.

W Uh, yeah. Head south and go past the roller coasters. Then turn left and walk past the gift shop.

M So they're near the gift shop?

W Yeah, between that and the snack stands.

| Vocabulary | spill 쏟다   head ~로 향하다 .   south 남쪽   snack stand 간이 식당 |

남 얘야, 화장실이 어딘지 알고 있니? 내가 셔츠에 소다를 쏟았구나.

여 네. 남쪽으로 가서 롤러 코스터를 지나세요. 그런 다음 왼쪽으로 돌아 선물 가게를 지나요.

남 그럼 화장실이 선물 가게 근처에 있다는 거니?

여 네, 선물 가게와 간이 식당 사이에요.

M Excuse me, miss. Could you help me for just a second?

W Sure. What do you need?

M Could you tell me where the Tyson Shipping Offices are? I have an interview for a part-time job there in ten minutes.

W Oh, sorry, but I'm not familiar with this area.

남 실례합니다. 잠깐만 도와주시겠어요?

여 물론이죠. 무엇 때문에 그러세요?

남 Tyson Shipping 사무실이 어딘지 아세요? 전 10분 뒤에 그 곳에서 아르바이트 면접이 있거든요.

여 오, 죄송하지만 저도 이 지역은 잘 몰라요.

W Is this bus heading for South Market?

M Yeah. We should get there in about 30 minutes.

W But that will be 8:30! We need to get there by 8:15. Danny will be waiting for us.

M Oh, we should have taken bus 443, then.

W What? Isn't this bus 443?

M No, this is bus 433.

W Oh, no! Hurry up. Let's get off at the next stop and transfer to bus 443.

M OK.

여 이 버스가 South Market으로 가니?

남 응. 우린 약 30분 후에 그 곳에 도착할 거야.

여 하지만 그럼 8시 반이 되잖아! 우린 그 곳에 8시 15분까지 가야 해. Danny가 우릴 기다릴 텐데.

남 오, 우린 그럼 443번 버스를 탔어야 했어.

여 뭐? 이 버스가 443번이 아냐?

남 아니, 이 버스는 433번이야.

여 오, 이런! 서둘러. 다음 역에서 내려서 443번으로 갈아타자.

남 그래.

W Good afternoon, ladies and gentlemen. This is your pilot speaking. Our plane is scheduled to land in New York at 6:30 p.m. This will be a four-hour flight. We will serve snacks at 4:00 p.m., and we will start our in-flight movie at 4:30 p.m. If you have any other questions, please ask a flight attendant. Thank you.

여 안녕하십니까, 신사 숙녀 여러분. 저는 기장입니다. 우리 비행기는 오후 6시 30분에 뉴욕에 도착할 예정입니다. 4시간 비행이 될 것입니다. 저희는 오후 4시에 간식을 제공해 드리며, 4시 30분에 영화를 시작할 것입니다. 다른 질문 사항이 있으시면 승무원에게 질문하십시오. 감사합니다.

W Hey, can you tell me <u>how to get</u> to the Hilton Hotel?

M Yeah. <u>Take this train</u> to the West Avenue station. Then take the Southbound train to Baltimore Station. From there <u>you walk north</u> to the hotel.

W Okay. How far <u>of a walk</u> is it?

M It's <u>about three blocks</u>.

W Thank you very much.

Vocabulary	north 북쪽 far 먼

여 얘야, 힐튼 호텔로 가는 길을 말해 주겠니?

남 네. 이 기차를 타셔서 West Avenue 역으로 가세요. 그런 다음 Southbound 기차를 타서 Baltimore 역으로 가세요. 거기서 북쪽으로 호텔까지 걸어가면 되요.

여 그렇구나. 얼마나 걸어야 하니?

남 세 블록 정도요.

여 정말 고맙구나.

M Hey, <u>you look lost</u>. Do you need some help?

W Oh, yes, please. I'm <u>new to this school</u>, so I don't know where anything is.

M Where do you <u>want to go</u>?

W I want to know where <u>the computer lab is</u>.

Vocabulary	lost 길을 잃은 computer lab 컴퓨터실

남 얘. 너 길을 잃은 것 같구나. 도움이 필요하니?

여 아. 그래. 난 이 학교 전학생이라서 어디가 어딘지 모르겠어.

남 어디 가려고 하는데?

여 난 컴퓨터실이 어딘지 알고 싶어.

 **Check Up** p.43

01 a → c → b **02** b, c

03 A Do you know how to make a computer program?

B Uh, not really. I'm not good at making computer programs.

A Aw. I want to make a program for a video game, but I have no idea how to begin.

B You know, I have a friend who's good at that stuff. He could possibly help you.

Check Up Scripts

01

W	Wow. It sure is raining a lot today, isn't it?	여	와. 오늘 정말 비가 많이 온다, 그렇지 않니?
M	Yeah, I guess it's no surprise, though. It was really cloudy yesterday.	남	그러게. 하지만 놀라운 일은 아닌 것 같아. 어제 정말 구름이 잔뜩 끼었었거든.
W	Yeah, you're right. Still, it's been raining so much for the past week. Maybe we can't go hiking tomorrow.	여	그래, 맞아. 그래도 지난 주부터 비가 계속 많이 오네. 어쩌면 우리 내일 하이킹을 못 가겠어.
M	Well, the weather forecast said it should be pretty clear and sunny tomorrow.	남	음, 일기예보에서 내일은 아주 맑고 햇빛이 난다고 했어.

Vocabulary	surprise 놀라운 일 cloudy 구름 낀 still 하지만 go hiking 하이킹 가다 weather forecast 일기 예보 pretty 아주, 꽤 clear 맑은

02

M	Hey, Jessica. Let's go outside and do something exciting. Are you good at tennis?	남	얘, Jessica. 우리 밖에 나가서 뭔가 신나는 일을 하자. 넌 테니스를 잘하니?
W	No, I'm not. I've never played tennis.	여	아니. 난 테니스 쳐 본 적 없어.
M	Then how about badminton?	남	그럼 배드민턴은 어때?
W	Well, I know how to play badminton, but I don't really like it. How about going swimming?	여	음. 배드민턴 치는 법은 알지만 별로 좋아하지 않아. 수영 가는 게 어때?
M	Oh, can you swim?	남	아, 너 수영할 줄 아니?
W	Yeah. Let's go.	여	응. 가자.

Vocabulary	exciting 신나는 be good at ~을 잘하다

03

A	Do you know how to make a computer program?	A	넌 컴퓨터 프로그램을 어떻게 만드는지 아니?
B	Uh, not really. I'm not good at making computer programs.	B	아, 아니. 난 컴퓨터 프로그램 만드는 것을 잘 못해.

A Aw. I want to make a program for a video game, but I have no idea how to begin.

B You know, I have a friend who's good at that stuff. He could possibly help you.

A 이런. 난 비디오 게임을 위한 프로그램을 만들고 싶은데, 어떻게 시작해야 할지 모르겠어.

B 있잖아. 내겐 그런 일에 능한 친구가 하나 있어. 걔가 아마 널 도울 수 있을 거야.

Actual Test　　1 ④　2 ③　3 ①　4 ②　5 ⑤　6 ③　7 ④　8 ②　　| p.44

M Hey, Clarice, do you want to go see a movie with me on Wednesday night?

W Oh, sorry, Louis. I have band practice that night.

M Oh, I see. Well, how about Friday night, then?

W I can't. I go rock climbing early Saturday morning, so I can't go out then.

M Oh. Well when will you be free?

W Hmm. I'm not busy Sunday afternoon.

남 안녕. Clarice. 너 수요일 밤에 나랑 영화 보러 갈래?

여 아. 미안해. Louis. 난 그 날 밤에 밴드 연습이 있어.

남 아. 그렇구나. 그럼 금요일 밤은 어때?

여 안돼. 난 토요일 아침 일찍 암벽 등반을 가거든. 그래서 안돼.

남 아, 그럼 언제 한가하니?

여 음. 일요일 오후엔 바쁘지 않아.

① **W** Danny, can you ski? I want to learn how to ski.

　M Oh, yes, I can teach you.

② **W** Are you good at math?

　M Yeah, I usually get a perfect score on math tests.

③ **W** Do you know how to use this fax machine?

　M Peggy said she will send you the fax.

④ **W** Can you make six dresses by Friday?

　M That's impossible. I need at least a week to do that.

⑤ **W** Do you think Mr. Black will fire Karen?

　M It's possible. She hasn't done much work lately.

① **여** Danny. 너 스키 탈 수 있니? 난 스키 타는 법을 배우고 싶어.

　남 오, 그럼 내가 널 가르쳐 줄 수 있어.

② **여** 넌 수학을 잘하니?

　남 응. 난 수학 시험에서 보통 완벽한 점수를 받지.

③ **여** 이 팩스 기계 어떻게 사용하는지 아니?

　남 Peggy가 네게 팩스를 보낼 거라고 했어.

④ **여** 금요일까지 6벌의 드레스를 만들 수 있나요?

　남 불가능해요. 그걸 하려면 적어도 1주일은 필요해요.

⑤ **여** 넌 Black씨가 Karen을 해고할 거라고 생각하니?

　남 가능하지. 그녀는 최근 일을 너무 안 했어.

3

M Hey, Allison. Do you have a minute?

W Sure, Bill. What's up?

M Well, we're going to be really busy on Saturday. I was wondering if you could possibly come in to help.

W Uh, sorry, but I don't think I can. My sister and I are going to the beach this weekend. Besides, I've already worked 3 extra days for our club this week.

M Oh, I didn't know that. Don't worry about it, then.

남 저, Allison. 잠깐 시간 있니?

여 그럼, Bill. 무슨 일이야?

남 음, 우린 토요일에 정말 바빠질 거야. 혹시 네가 토요일에 도와주러 올 수 있는지 궁금해서.

여 아, 미안하지만 안될 것 같아. 여동생과 난 이번 주말에 해변에 갈 거야. 게다가, 난 이미 이번 주에 우리 동아리를 위해 3일이나 더 일했어.

남 아, 몰랐어. 그럼 걱정하지 마.

4

W Can I talk to you, Mr. Baker?

M Sure. What is it, Helen?

W I feel like our team lost yesterday because of me. I think I should quit.

M Oh, Helen. Don't say that. It wasn't your fault.

W But I'm not good at volleyball at all.

M That's not true. You are a hard worker, and you've been a great help to our team.

여 잠깐 말씀 좀 드릴 수 있을까요, Baker 선생님?

남 그럼. 무슨 일이니, Helen?

여 전 우리 팀이 어제 저 때문에 진 것 같아요. 제가 팀을 그만둬야 할 것 같아요.

남 오, Helen. 그렇게 말하지 마. 그건 네 잘못이 아니었어.

여 하지만 전 배구를 전혀 잘하지 못하는 걸요.

남 그건 사실이 아니야. 넌 정말 노력하는 선수이고, 우리 팀에 대단한 도움이 되고 있단다.

5

M Today was a happy day in West Virginia. Twelve miners were saved from almost certain death. A week ago they became trapped inside the tunnel. They had no food or water, and they had very little air to breathe. Fortunately, however, all twelve are alive. They have all returned to their families, who never gave up hope.

남 오늘은 West Virginia의 기쁜 날입니다. 12명의 광부들이 거의 죽음에 이르렀다가 구조되었습니다. 1주일 전, 그들은 터널 속에 갇히게 되었습니다. 그들은 먹을 음식이나 물도 없었고, 숨쉴 수 있는 공기도 거의 없었습니다. 하지만 다행스럽게도, 12명 모두 생존했습니다. 그들은 결코 희망을 포기하지 않았던 그들의 가족의 곁으로 돌아갔습니다.

M Hey, Carol. I heard that you're getting married. Congratulations!

W Oh, thank you, Dave. Can you come to my wedding?

M When is it?

W It's the third Sunday of June.

M Sure, I can. I'll bring a special gift for you.

W Thank you.

Vocabulary	get married 결혼하다　Congratulations. 축하해.　wedding 결혼식　gift 선물

남 얘, Carol. 난 네가 결혼한다고 들었어. 축하해!

여 오, 고마워, Dave. 내 결혼식에 올 수 있니?

남 언젠데?

여 6월의 세 번째 일요일이야.

남 그럼 갈 수 있지. 너를 위한 특별한 선물을 가져 갈게.

여 고마워.

M Excuse me. Is the public pool open?

W Oh, yes, but you can't come in.

M What? Why?

W There's a private party at the pool today. Only invited guests are allowed in. You'll have to come back to the pool tomorrow.

M It's not fair! I have to go to school tomorrow and I'll have to wait an entire week to go swimming!

Vocabulary	pool 수영장　private 개인의　invited 초대받은　allow 허락하다　fair 공평한　entire 전체의

남 실례합니다. 수영장이 문을 연 건가요?

여 아, 네. 하지만 들어오실 수 없습니다.

남 네? 왜요?

여 오늘 수영장에서 개인 파티가 있어서요. 초대받은 손님들만 들어가실 수 있습니다. 당신은 내일 오셔야 할 것 같아요.

남 불공평하군요! 전 내일 학교를 가야 하기 때문에 수영을 하려면 일주일 내내 기다려야 한다구요!

W Good morning, everyone. Welcome to Freshman Chemistry. There are just a few simple rules for this course. First, you will do homework every night. Second, you will have a quiz or test every Friday. You will also have to write three papers, and you will have one group project. Don't worry, though. This class will be difficult, but it will not be impossible.

Vocabulary	freshman 신입생　chemistry 화학　rule 규칙

여 안녕하세요, 여러분. Freshman Chemistry를 듣게 되신 것을 환영합니다. 이 코스에서는 단지 몇 가지 간단한 규칙들이 있어요. 우선, 여러분은 매일 밤 숙제를 해야 합니다. 둘째로, 여러분은 매주 금요일에는 퀴즈나 테스트를 봐야 합니다. 그리고 세 개의 보고서를 써야 하고, 하나의 그룹 프로젝트를 할 것입니다. 하지만 걱정하지 마세요. 이 수업은 어렵지만 불가능한 수업은 아니니까요.

UNIT VIII HOW OFTEN DO YOU SWIM?

Check Up

01 1. c 2. a **02** 1. inline skating 2. once a week

03 **A** Peggy, I heard you have many puppies. How many puppies do you have?

B I have eight puppies.

A How often do you feed them a day?

B I feed them three times a day.

Check Up Scripts

01

W Tim, do you like to go see movies?

M Yeah. I really love to. I usually go see a movie every weekend.

W What kind of movies do you like?

M I like horror movies. Let's go see a horror movie sometime.

W Oh, I don't like scary movies. I like action movies.

여 Tim, 넌 영화 보러 가는 것을 좋아하니?

남 그래. 난 정말 좋아해. 난 보통 매 주말 마다 영화를 보러 가.

여 넌 어떤 종류의 영화를 좋아하니?

남 난 공포 영화를 좋아해. 다음에 공포 영화를 보러 가자.

여 아. 난 무서운 영화를 좋아하지 않아. 난 액션 영화가 좋아.

Vocabulary	horror 공포　　sometime 언젠가　　scary 무서운

02

M I love spending time outside on nice days.

W Yeah, me too. What is your favorite outdoor activity?

M Hmm. Riding on my inline skates is my favorite activity. What about you?

W I love swimming myself.

M That's cool. How often do you swim?

W About once a week.

남 난 날이 좋은 날 밖에서 시간을 보내는 것을 좋아해.

여 나도 그래. 넌 어떤 야외 활동을 가장 좋아하니?

남 음. 인라인 스케이트 타는 것이 내가 가장 좋아하는 야외 활동이야. 너는?

여 난 수영을 좋아해.

남 멋진데. 넌 얼마나 자주 수영하니?

여 일주일에 한번 정도 수영해.

Vocabulary	spend 시간을 보내다　　outdoor 야외의　　activity 활동

03

A Peggy, I heard you have many puppies. How many puppies do you have?

B I have eight puppies.

A How often do you feed them a day?

B I feed them three times a day.

A Peggy, 난 네가 강아지를 많이 키우고 있다고 들었어. 몇 마리나 가지고 있니?

B 내겐 8마리의 강아지가 있어.

A 하루에 몇 번 먹이를 주니?

B 하루에 3번 씩 먹이를 줘.

Vocabulary	puppy 강아지　　feed 먹이를 주다

1

W Leo, did you have a good weekend?

M Yeah, I had a good time with my girlfriend.

W What did you do?

M I wanted to go to an amusement park, but my girlfriend didn't want to. So we went to the new city zoo instead.

W Was it crowded?

M Yeah, but we had a lot of fun. The best thing there was the panda bear.

여 Leo, 즐거운 주말 보냈니?

남 응. 난 내 여자친구와 즐거운 시간을 보냈어.

여 뭘 했는데?

남 난 놀이동산에 가고 싶었는데, 내 여자친구가 가기 싫다고 했어. 그래서 대신 우린 새로 생긴 시립 동물원에 갔지.

여 사람들로 붐볐니?

남 응. 하지만 재미있었어. 그 곳의 최고 멋진 동물은 팬더곰이었어.

| Vocabulary | amusement park 놀이동산   instead 대신   crowded 붐비는 |

2

M Oh, you have a lot of books, Kate!

W Yeah, I like to read, so I often go to the bookstore and buy books.

M How many books do you read a month?

W About 10, I think.

M Really? You read twice as many books as me.

남 아. 넌 정말 많은 책을 가지고 있구나, Kate!

여 그래. 난 책 읽는 것을 좋아해서 종종 서점에 들러 책을 사.

남 한 달에 몇 권의 책을 읽니?

여 10권 정도인 것 같아.

남 정말? 넌 내가 읽는 책의 두 배나 읽는 구나.

| Vocabulary | twice 2배 |

3

W I can't believe this! I just got off my plane at the airport, but I can't go anywhere! There's a terrible snowstorm outside, and almost all the roads are closed. I've already waited for four hours for my dad to come pick me up. How much longer will the wait be? I just want to get out of here and take a long nap.

여 이 사실을 믿을 수가 없어! 내가 방금 공항의 비행기에서 내렸는데, 어디에도 갈 수가 없다. 밖에는 심한 눈보라가 휘날리고, 거의 모든 길이 폐쇄되었다. 난 아빠가 데리러 오기를 네 시간째 기다렸다. 이 기다림이 얼마나 더 오래될까? 난 그저 여기서 벗어나서 긴 낮잠을 자고 싶을 뿐이다.

| Vocabulary | get off 내리다   snowstorm 눈보라   pick up 마중 나오다   take a nap 낮잠을 자다 |

4

M Hey, Claire! How's it going?

남 얘. Claire! 어떻게 지내니?

W I'm doing OK, Ryan. I didn't know you exercised here.

M Yeah. I lift weights here.

W Really? I've never seen you here before. How often do you exercise?

M Three times a week. How about you?

W I come here once a week.

Question How often does the man exercise?

여 난 잘 지내, Ryan. 난 네가 여기서 운동하는지 몰랐는데.

남 응. 난 여기서 역기를 들어.

여 정말? 난 전에 이곳에서 널 본 적이 없어. 얼마나 자주 운동을 하니?

남 일주일에 3번. 넌?

여 난 일주일에 한 번 이곳에 와.

질문 남자는 얼마나 자주 운동을 하나요?

<table><tr><td>Vocabulary</td><td>lift 들어올리다   weight 역기</td></tr></table>

5

M ① The man spends the most time studying math.

② The man studies English and history for the same amount of time.

③ The man spends the least time studying science.

④ The man studies math for more than two hours.

⑤ The man studies history for less than two hours.

남 ① 남자는 수학을 공부하면서 가장 많은 시간을 보낸다.

② 남자는 영어와 역사를 같은 양의 시간 동안 공부한다.

③ 남자는 과학을 공부하면서 가장 적은 시간을 보낸다.

④ 남자는 수학을 2시간 이상 공부한다.

⑤ 남자는 역사를 2시간 미만 공부한다.

<table><tr><td>Vocabulary</td><td>same 똑 같은   amount 양   least 가장 적은</td></tr></table>

6

W Excuse me, Mr. Davis?

M Oh, good morning, Cathy. Come in. What's on your mind?

W Well, sir, I was wondering if I could take some time off work next month.

M How much time would you like off?

W Three days, sir. From Wednesday, October 6th to Friday, October 8th.

M Okay.

여 실례합니다, Davis씨?

남 아, 좋은 아침이에요, Cathy. 들어와요. 무슨 일이죠?

여 음, 저 다음 달에 휴가를 쓸 수 있을지 궁금해서요.

남 얼마나 쓰려고 하는데요?

여 3일이요. 10월 6일 수요일부터 10월 8일 금요일까지요.

남 좋아요.

<table><tr><td>Vocabulary</td><td>mind 마음   take time off (from work) 휴직하다</td></tr></table>

7

① W What's the problem?

   M I have a high fever and I cough a lot.

② W Did you drop by the pharmacy?

① 여 무엇이 문제인가요?

   남 전 열이 높고, 기침을 자주 해요.

② 여 약국에 들렀나요?

M	Yes, I bought some medicine for a sore throat.	남	네. 전 아픈 목을 낫게 하는 약을 샀어요.
③ W	Let me take a look at your arm. Does it hurt?	③ 여	네 팔을 좀 보자꾸나. 아프니?
M	Yes, I think it's broken.	남	네. 부러진 것 같아요.
④ W	Don't forget to take this medicine three times a day.	④ 여	이 약을 하루에 세 번 먹는 것을 잊지 않도록 하거라.
M	Okay, I won't.	남	네. 그럴게요.
⑤ W	Hey, you look terrible. I think you should go see a doctor.	⑤ 여	얘. 너 안 좋아 보인다. 병원에 가야 할 것 같아.
M	Okay. Could you drive me to the hospital?	남	응. 병원까지 좀 태워 줄래?

Vocabulary	fever 열 cough 기침하다 drop by 들르다 pharmacy 약국 sore 아픈 throat 목

M	How can I help you today, ma'am?	남	어떻게 도와드릴까요. 부인?
W	It's my car. I was driving the other day, and it started shaking a lot.	여	제 차 때문에요. 지난 번에 운전을 하고 있었는데 많이 덜컹거리기 시작했어요.
M	Did you have a flat tire?	남	타이어에 펑크가 났나요?
W	No, the tires are fine. I think there may be something wrong with the engine.	여	아니오, 타이어는 멀쩡해요. 전 엔진에 문제가 있는 것 같다고 생각해요.
M	I see. We'll take a look at it.	남	그렇군요. 저희가 살펴 보겠습니다.
W	Thank you. How many days will it take to fix the problem?	여	감사합니다. 문제점을 고치는 데 얼마나 걸릴까요?

Vocabulary	shake 흔들다 flat tire 펑크난 타이어 engine 엔진 fix 고치다

UNIT IX YOU'D BETTER HURRY UP.

✿ Check Up

01 a **02** 1. a, d   2. b, c

03 **A** Ron, <u>what should I do</u> to lose weight?

   B <u>I think you should</u> stop eating junk food.

   A Okay. And what else?

   B <u>You'd better exercise</u> every day.

   A <u>That's a good idea</u>. Thank you.

Check Up Scripts

01

W Honey, you said you are going to see a basketball game, right?

M Yeah. I'm so excited!

W What time does the game start?

M At 6:00.

W You'd better hurry up then. You should leave here by 5:00.

M Oh, that only gives me 20 minutes to get ready!

여	얘야, 농구 경기를 보러 간다고 했지, 그렇지?
남	네, 너무 신나요!
여	경기가 몇 시에 시작하니?
남	6시요.
여	그렇다면 서두르는 것이 좋겠구나. 5시까지는 출발해야만해.
남	오, 그럼 준비할 시간이 20분 밖에 되지 않네요!

> **Vocabulary**   get ready 준비하다

02

W Kevin, how can you play video games all day? It's such a waste of time.

M They're fun! Have you ever tried playing video games?

W Absolutely not. I think you'd better not play them, either. It's really harmful to your mind.

M Hmm. I don't think so, Jean. It's a great way to both relieve stress and make lots of new friends.

여	Kevin, 넌 어떻게 하루 종일 비디오 게임을 할 수 있니? 그건 시간 낭비야.
남	비디오 게임은 재미있어! 해본 적 없니?
여	전혀 없지. 난 네가 비디오 게임을 하지 않는 것이 좋을 거라 생각해. 네 정신 건강에 해로워.
남	음. 난 그렇게 생각하지 않아, Jean. 비디오 게임은 스트레스를 풀어주고 새로운 친구를 사귀게 해 주는 좋은 수단이야.

> **Vocabulary**   waste 낭비   absolutely 전적으로, 전혀   harmful 해로운   relieve 해소하다   stress 스트레스
> make friends 친구를 사귀다

03

A Ron, what should I do to lose weight?

B I think you should stop eating junk food.

A Okay. And what else?

A	Ron, 살을 빼려면 어떻게 해야 할까?
B	난 네가 정크 푸드를 그만 먹어야 한다고 생각해.
A	그래. 그리고 다른 건?

B You'd better exercise every day.

A That's a good idea. Thank you.

| Vocabulary | lose weight 살을 빼다   junk food 정크 푸드 (칼로리는 높고 영양가 없는 음식) |

Actual Test   1 ②   2 ①   3 ③   4 ④   5 ①   6 ⑤   7 ②   8 ④ | p.56

M To get this job, you should get a lot of hard training. You should be very tough and smart if you want to do it. You also need to study a lot of different sciences and learn how to fly space shuttles. It is a very difficult job. That's why most people can't do it.

남 이 직업을 갖기 위해서, 당신은 호된 훈련을 많이 받아야 합니다. 그것이 되기 위해서 당신은 매우 강하고 똑똑해야 합니다. 그리고 여러 과학 분야에 대해 많이 공부해야 하며, 우주선이 어떻게 나는지 알아야 합니다. 그것은 아주 어려운 직업입니다. 그래서 대부분의 사람들이 그 일을 할 수 없습니다.

| Vocabulary | training 훈련   tough 강한   smart 똑똑한   space shuttle 우주선 |

M Ms. Ellen? I need some help.

W Sure Paul. What's on your mind?

M All my friends have a dream, but I have no idea what I want to do when I grow up.

W Paul, you're only 15. Don't worry too much.

M Yeah, but I'd still like some ideas.

W Well, you're a good speaker, and you're very smart. I think you should consider studying law.

M That's something to think about. Thanks.

남 Ellen 선생님? 도움이 필요해요.

여 그래, Paul. 무슨 일이니?

남 제 친구들 모두에겐 꿈이 있는데, 전 제가 나중에 커서 무엇을 하고 싶은지 모르겠어요.

여 Paul, 넌 아직 15살이잖니. 너무 걱정하지 마.

남 네, 하지만 의견을 좀 주시면 좋겠어요.

여 음. 넌 훌륭한 연설가이고, 아주 똑똑하지. 난 네가 법을 공부하는 것을 고려해보는 게 좋을 것 같아.

남 생각해 볼 만 하네요. 감사해요.

| Vocabulary | grow up 성장하다   consider 고려하다   law 법 |

[The answering machine beeps.]

M Hello, Ms. Park? This is Allen Smith. I am returning your call from yesterday. I am honored that your magazine wants to interview me. If you like, you can interview me at my office around 10:30 a.m. this Friday. You should get here earlier than that, though. It can be

[자동응답기 소리]

남 안녕하세요. Ms. Park. Allen Smith입니다. 어제 전화 주셨지요. 당신의 잡지사가 저를 인터뷰하겠다고 하시니 영광입니다. 원하신다면 이번 금요일 오전 10시 30분쯤에 저의 사무실에서 인터뷰가 가능합니다. 그런데 이 곳에 그 보다 더 일찍 오시는 것이 좋을 겁니다. 9시 이후에는 주차 공간을 찾기가 어려울 수 있으니까요. 그럼 그때 뵐 수 있길 바

difficult to find a parking space here after 9:00. I hope to see you then!

랍니다!

① M I have a terrible headache.

W I think you should take some aspirin.

② M I lost my brother's favorite book. What should I do?

W You'd better be honest with him.

③ M Do you think I should quit my job?

W Well, I think it's not a good idea.

④ M What should I do to stay healthy?

W I think you can do well.

⑤ M You'd better not stay up all night.

W Yeah, I think you're right.

① 남 난 두통이 너무 심해.

여 난 네가 아스피린을 좀 먹어야 한다고 생각해.

② 남 난 형이 가장 좋아하는 책을 잃어버렸어. 어떻게 해야 하지?

여 솔직히 말해야 한다고 생각해.

③ 남 넌 내가 일을 그만두어야 한다고 생각하니?

여 음. 그건 좋은 생각이 아닌 것 같아.

④ 남 건강을 유지하려면 어떻게 해야 할까?

여 난 네가 잘 할 수 있다고 생각해.

⑤ 남 넌 밤새 깨어 있지 않는 것이 좋아.

여 응. 난 네가 옳다고 생각해.

W Thomas. You look terrible. What's wrong?

M My tooth really aches. It's painful.

W Oh, that's too bad. I think you should go see a dentist right away.

M It will be OK after some time.

W Thomas, if you don't go see a dentist now, the problem will keep getting worse and worse. You might have to pull the tooth out.

M Yeah, you're right.

여 Thomas. 넌 아주 안 좋아 보여. 무슨 일이니?

남 이가 너무 아파. 고통스러워.

여 아. 안됐구나. 난 네가 당장 치과에 가야 한다고 생각해.

남 시간이 좀 지나면 괜찮아 질 거야.

여 Thomas. 지금 치과에 가지 않으면 문제는 더욱 더 심해질 거야. 넌 이를 뽑아야 할지도 몰라.

남 그래. 네가 맞아.

W Hey, Walter. How's it going?

M I'm feeling pretty good today. I just bought a plane ticket to New Orleans for next month.

W Oh, cool! Are you going to the big festival there?

M I sure am. I just need to find a hotel to

여 안녕. Walter. 잘 지내?

남 난 오늘 꽤 기분이 좋아. 난 방금 다음달에 New Orleans로 가는 비행기표를 샀거든.

여 오, 멋진데! 거기서 하는 성대한 축제도 갈거니?

남 물론 그래야지. 난 그 곳에서 머물 수 있는 호텔을 찾아

stay in.

W Yeah, you'd better <u>make a reservation</u> as soon as possible. Otherwise, you <u>might</u> <u>not find</u> a <u>hotel</u> in time.

M I know, I know. If I can't, it's no problem, though. I can stay <u>at my uncle's house</u> there.

여 응. 넌 가능한 빨리 예약을 해 두는 게 좋을 거야. 그렇지 않으면 제 시간에 호텔을 찾을 수 없을지도 몰라.

남 알아. 알아. 하지만 만약 호텔을 못 잡아도, 문제가 되지는 않아. 그 곳에 있는 삼촌 댁에 머무르면 되거든.

Vocabulary	festival 축제 make a reservation 예약하다 as soon as possible 가능한 빨리 otherwise 그렇지 않으면

7

W Hey, Mitch, <u>you look down</u>. What's the problem?

M I asked Sandra out on a date, but she said no. I <u>don't understand why</u>.

W I have an idea. It could be the way you look.

M <u>What's wrong with</u> how I look?

W Well, it's just that you'll be popular with girls if you <u>try to look tidy</u>. For example, I think you should get a nice haircut.

M Well, I could <u>give it a try</u>.

여 얘. Mitch. 너 기분이 안 좋아 보여. 문제가 뭐니?

남 난 Sandra에게 데이트 신청을 했는데 그녀가 거절했어. 난 이유를 모르겠어.

여 내게 좋은 생각이 있어. 네 외모 때문일지도 몰라.

남 내 외모가 어때서?

여 음. 네가 더 단정해 보이려고 노력한다면 여자애들에게 인기가 있을 거라는 뜻이야. 예를 들어, 난 네가 머리를 깔끔하게 잘라야 한다고 생각해.

남 음. 시도를 해 볼게.

Vocabulary	down 기분이 나쁜 ask someone out on a date ~에게 데이트 신청을 하다 popular 인기 있는 tidy 단정한 haircut 이발

8

W Hey, Jason? Peggy's birthday is this Friday.

M Oh. It is?

W Yeah. She's having <u>a big party</u> and she wants you to come. <u>Can you make it</u>?

M I'm afraid I can't. I already <u>have other plans</u>.

W Well, that's too bad. <u>You'd better call her</u> and wish her a happy birthday, though. I'm sure <u>she'd appreciate that</u>.

여 Jason. Peggy의 생일이 이번 주 금요일이야.

남 아. 그래?

여 응. 그녀는 성대한 파티를 열 예정인데, 네가 오길 원해. 올 수 있니?

남 유감이지만 못 가. 난 다른 계획이 이미 있거든.

여 음. 안됐구나. 그렇지만 전화를 해서 생일 축하한다고 전해 주는 게 좋을 것 같아. 난 그녀가 고마워할 거라고 확신해.

Vocabulary	afraid 유감스러운 already 이미 had better ~하는 것이 낫다 appreciate 고마워하다

UNIT X ARE YOU INTERESTED IN ART?

✹ Check Up

p.61

01 a **02** a, c

03 **A** Ron, <u>are you interested in</u> rock music?

　　B Oh, sorry, but I <u>don't have much interest in</u> rock.

　　A <u>What are you interested in</u> then?

　　B <u>I am interested in pop music</u>, and my favorite singer is Mariah Carey.

Check Up Scripts

01

M Hey, Kate. Are you interested in art?

W Yes, I'm really interested in art.

M How about going to the art gallery this weekend? They're exhibiting many famous artists' paintings, like some by Van Gogh.

W Sounds great.

남 이봐, Kate. 너 미술에 관심 있니?

여 응. 난 미술에 관심이 많아.

남 이번 주말에 미술관에 같이 가는 게 어떠니? 미술관에서 Van Gogh와 같은 유명한 화가의 그림들을 전시한대.

여 멋지구나.

Vocabulary	be interested in ~에 관심이 있다　art gallery 미술관　exhibit 전시하다　famous 유명한 artist 화가

02

W Jeremy, are you interested in acting?

M Yeah, I really am.

W Then how about acting in our school play?

M Sounds interesting. I've always wanted to try acting.

W Well, all you have to do is learn a few lines and audition for the play next Wednesday.

M Great! I'll definitely give it a shot.

여 Jeremy, 너는 연기에 관심이 있니?

남 응. 관심 많아.

여 그럼 우리 학교 연극에서 연기해 보는 게 어때?

남 흥미로운걸. 난 언제나 연기를 해보고 싶었거든.

여 음. 네가 해야 하는 일은 대사 몇 줄을 외우고 다음 주 수요일에 연극을 위한 오디션을 보는 거야.

남 좋아! 난 꼭 해 보겠어.

Vocabulary	act 연기하다　line 대사　audition 오디션을 보다　definitely 꼭, 확실히　shot 시도

03

A Ron, are you interested in rock music?

B Oh, sorry, but I don't have much interest in rock.

A What are you interested in then?

B I am interested in pop music, and my favorite singer is Mariah Carey.

A Ron, 너 록음악에 관심 있니?

B 아, 미안하지만 난 록에 그다지 관심이 없어.

A 그럼 무엇에 관심 있니?

B 난 팝 음악에 관심이 있고, 내가 가장 좋아하는 가수는 Mariah Carey야.

Vocabulary	interest 관심

Actual Test   1 ⑤   2 ①   3 ⑤   4 ①   5 ③   6 ②   7 ④   8 ③ | p.62

1

① **W** Hey, do you know where my tennis rackets are?

   M I have no idea.

② **W** Wow. There are many club posters here.

   M Yeah, I don't know which one to choose.

③ **W** I'm really bored. Let's go outside.

   M Oh, but it's too hot outside. Let's just stay home.

④ **W** Are you interested in seeing this movie, dear?

   M No. I heard it wasn't that good.

⑤ **W** Ted, let's join this tennis club.

   M Well, I'm not really interested in tennis.

① **여** 넌 내 테니스 라켓이 어디 있는지 알고 있니?

   남 모르겠는데.

② **여** 와. 이 곳에는 정말 많은 클럽 포스터가 있구나.

   남 응. 난 어떤 것을 선택해야 할 지 모르겠어.

③ **여** 난 정말 지루해. 밖에 나가자.

   남 아. 밖은 너무 더워. 그냥 집에 있자.

④ **여** 이 영화에 관심 있니?

   남 아니. 난 그 영화 별로라고 들었어.

⑤ **여** Ted, 이 테니스 클럽에 가입하자.

   남 글쎄. 난 테니스에 별로 관심이 없어.

> **Vocabulary**   tennis racket 테니스 라켓   poster 포스터   choose 선택하다   bored 지루한   join 가입하다

2

W Hey, Edward, are you interested in seeing a romantic comedy?

M What? No, I hate romantic comedies.

W You do? I love them. They are my favorite kind of movie.

M Not for me. I think they're too boring.

W What kinds of movies do you like to watch then?

M I enjoy watching science fiction movies.

여 Edward, 넌 로맨틱 코미디 보는 것에 관심 있니?

남 뭐? 아니. 난 로맨틱 코미디가 싫어.

여 그래? 난 좋아하는데. 그건 내가 가장 좋아하는 영화 장르야.

남 내겐 아니야. 난 그것이 너무 지루하다고 생각해.

여 그럼 넌 무슨 영화 보길 좋아하니?

남 난 공상 과학 영화를 보는 것을 좋아해.

> **Vocabulary**   romantic comedy 로맨틱 코미디   science fiction 공상 과학 영화

3

M Hey, Dora. Do you enjoy studying in the library?

W Actually, I do. It's nice and quiet in there. And all those books are really helpful.

M Hmm. Well, I don't study in there often.

남 얘, Dora. 넌 도서관에서 공부하기를 좋아하니?

여 사실 그래. 그 곳은 멋지고 조용하잖아. 그리고 모든 책들이 정말 유용하기도 하고.

남 흠. 글쎄. 난 도서관에서 자주 공부하지 않아.

W Why?	**여** 왜?
M I stay up late at night to study, and the library closes too early for me.	**남** 난 공부하기 위해 밤늦게까지 깨어있는데, 도서관은 너무 일찍 문을 닫잖아.
W I don't think that's a good study habit.	**여** 난 그것이 좋은 공부 습관이라고 생각하지 않아.

> **Vocabulary**   actually 사실   quiet 조용한   helpful 유용한   stay up late 늦게까지 깨어있다   habit 습관

4

W Danny, what are you reading?	**여** Danny, 넌 무엇을 읽고 있니?
M It's an article about new types of medicine.	**남** 새로운 약 종류에 관한 기사야.
W Oh, are you interested in medicine?	**여** 오, 넌 약에 관심이 있니?
M Yeah, I really am. I want to become a doctor when I'm older. But I don't really know what it takes to become one.	**남** 응, 난 정말 관심이 많아. 난 나중에 의사가 되고 싶어. 하지만 의사가 되기 위해 무엇을 해야 하는지 잘 모르겠어.
W Actually, my uncle is a doctor. I can ask him to give you some advice, if you'd like.	**여** 사실은 우리 삼촌께서 의사셔. 네가 원한다면 너에게 충고를 좀 해달라고 삼촌께 부탁 드려볼게.

> **Vocabulary**   article 기사   medicine 약   become ~이 되다   advice 충고

5

M Did you see the soccer game last night?	**남** 넌 어젯밤에 축구 경기를 보았니?
W Uh, I'm not really into soccer. In fact, I don't like sports at all.	**여** 음, 난 축구를 좋아하지 않아. 사실, 난 스포츠를 전혀 좋아하지 않아.
M Really? Well, what are you interested in?	**남** 정말? 음, 넌 무엇에 관심이 있는데?
W I really like going to concerts and plays with my friends. I especially like musicals.	**여** 난 친구들과 함께 콘서트와 연극을 보러 가는 것을 정말 좋아해. 특히 뮤지컬을 좋아하지.
M That's cool. Why don't we go see a musical sometime?	**남** 멋지네. 다음에 뮤지컬을 함께 보러 갈래?
W I'd love to.	**여** 물론.

> **Vocabulary**   be into something ~을 좋아하다   in fact 사실   especially 특히   sometime 언젠가

6

W Are you interested in buying some new shoes, Harold?	**여** 넌 새 신발을 사는 것에 관심 있니, Harold?
M No, I'm not interested in shoes. I already have two pairs. I do need to get a new pair of pants, though.	**남** 아니, 난 신발에 관심 없어. 난 이미 두 켤레나 있거든. 그런데 새 바지 한 벌은 필요해.
W Okay. How about some shirts?	**여** 그래. 셔츠는 어때?
M Uh, yeah. I should get two new shirts.	**남** 어, 그래. 난 새 셔츠 두 장이 필요해.
W Hey, check out this sweater! It feels really soft and comfortable.	**여** 이봐, 이 스웨터 좀 봐! 정말 부드럽고 편안한 느낌인데.

M But I don't like its color, and I don't think I need one. Let's go.	**남** 하지만 난 색깔이 마음에 안 들고, 필요하다고 생각하지 않아. 가자.

7

W Darren, are you going to the soccer game Friday night?	**여** Darren. 넌 금요일 밤에 축구 경기에 갈 거니?
M Oh, no. I'm not interested in sports. And I have plans on Friday. This really good jazz band's going to play at the Cotton Lounge.	**남** 아니. 난 운동에 관심이 없어. 그리고 금요일엔 계획이 있어. 정말 멋진 재즈 밴드들이 Cotton Lounge에서 연주를 할 거야.
W Oh. Are you interested in jazz music?	**여** 아, 너 재즈 음악에 관심이 있니?
M Yeah. I started listening to it about four years ago.	**남** 응. 난 4년 전부터 듣기 시작했어.
Question What is Darren interested in?	**질문** Darren은 무엇에 관심이 있나요?

8

M Rebecca, I just got this new kitten! She is so cute.	**남** Rebecca. 난 방금 새 아기고양이를 한 마리 얻었어! 너무 귀여워.
W Uh, that's nice.	**여** 아, 잘됐구나.
M Are you interested in seeing her sometime?	**남** 언젠가 보러 오겠니?
W Uh, no thanks. I'm not really interested in cats.	**여** 아, 됐어. 난 고양이에 관심이 별로 없거든.
M What? Why's that?	**남** 뭐? 왜?
W I just don't think they make good pets. I prefer dogs. They are very loyal and friendly, and they can protect you, too.	**여** 난 고양이가 좋은 애완동물이라고 생각하지 않아서 그래. 난 강아지를 더 좋아해. 강아지는 충성심 있고 다정하지. 그리고 너를 보호해 줄 수도 있고 말이야.

UNIT XI WHY DON'T YOU START JOGGING?

p.67

Check Up

01 b   **02** 1. find a good gift 2. shop online

03 A Derrick, why don't we have a group study tonight?

B I'd love to, but I have basketball practice tonight.

A How about tomorrow night? We can meet at my house.

B That's a good idea. Let's meet at 7 p.m.

Check Up Scripts

01

M How was the meal, ma'am?

W Everything was very good, thank you. I'd also like to try some dessert. Do you have any suggestions?

M How about our chocolate ice cream?

W Well, I tried that before, but I didn't think it was very good.

M Then how about our cheese cake?

W Okay, I'll try that.

남 부인, 식사는 어떠셨습니까?

여 모든 것이 훌륭했어요, 감사해요. 그리고 디저트를 좀 먹고 싶은데요. 추천할 만한 것이 있나요?

남 초콜릿 아이스크림은 어떠세요?

여 음, 전에 먹어본 적 있는데, 그다지 맛있지 않았어요.

남 그렇다면 치즈 케이크가 어떠세요?

여 그래요, 그걸로 먹을게요.

Vocabulary	meal 식사 suggestion 추천, 제안

02

W You look kind of worried, Peter. What's wrong?

M My mom's birthday is coming up, but I can't find a good gift for her. I've looked in every store I know, too!

W Why don't you shop online? There are tons of great things you can find.

M That's a great idea. It would save me a lot of trips, too.

여 너 좀 걱정스러워 보여, Peter. 무슨 일이니?

남 우리 엄마의 생일이 다가오고 있는데, 괜찮은 선물을 발견하지 못했어. 내가 알고 있는 모든 가게에 가 보았는데도!

여 온라인에서 쇼핑 해보는 것이 어때? 아주 좋은 물건들이 많아.

남 좋은 생각이네. 돌아다닐 필요도 없겠구나.

Vocabulary	tons of 아주 많은 save 절약하다

03

A Derrick, why don't we have a group study tonight?

B I'd love to, but I have basketball practice tonight.

A How about tomorrow night? We can meet at my house.

A Derrick, 오늘 밤에 그룹 스터디를 하는 게 어떠니?

B 그러고 싶은데, 난 오늘 밤 농구 연습이 있어.

A 내일 밤은 어때? 우리 집에서 만나자.

B That's a good idea. Let's meet at 7 p.m.

B 좋은 생각이네. 오후 7시에 만나자.

| Vocabulary | practice 연습 |

Actual Test

1 ④ 2 ② 3 ④ 4 ① 5 ① 6 ③ 7 ⑤ 8 ⑤ | p.68

1

[The telephone rings.]

W Hello, is Mr. Gibson there?

M This is Mr. Gibson. How <u>can I help you</u>?

W This is Amanda Preston. I'm with Carter Industries, and I'd like to <u>set up a job interview</u> with you.

M Oh, great! What time <u>shall we meet</u>?

W Any time after 1:00 p.m. on Wednesday would be best for me.

M Well, <u>how about 2: 30</u>?

W Okay. The interview will <u>take about 30 minutes</u>. I'll meet you then.

[전화벨 소리]

여 여보세요. Gibson씨 있나요?

남 전데요. 어떻게 도와드릴까요?

여 Amanda Preston입니다. 전 Carter Industries에 근무 중이고, 당신과 취업 면접 약속을 잡고 싶어서요.

남 아, 좋아요! 몇 시에 뵐까요?

여 수요일 오후 한 시 이후로 언제든 괜찮아요.

남 그럼, 2시 30분 어떠세요?

여 좋아요. 인터뷰는 약 30분 간 진행될 겁니다. 그 때 뵙도록 하죠.

| Vocabulary | set up (약속 등을) 정하다   take (시간이) ~걸리다 |

2

W Brian, are you <u>feeling any better</u> today?

M No, Mom, I still feel kind of sick. I <u>took some medicine</u>, but my head still hurts.

W Why don't you try <u>taking a nap</u> for a while? It might <u>help you recover</u> more quickly.

M I wish I could. But I have to <u>finish my homework first</u>.

여 Brian, 너 오늘은 좀 괜찮니?

남 아뇨, 엄마. 전 여전히 좀 아파요. 약을 좀 먹었는데, 머리가 여전히 아파요.

여 잠깐 낮잠을 자 보는 게 어떠니? 네가 더 빨리 나을 수 있도록 도와줄 거야.

남 그러고 싶어요. 그렇지만 먼저 숙제를 끝내야 해요.

| Vocabulary | take a nap 낮잠을 자다   for a while 잠깐 동안   recover 회복하다 |

3

[The answering machine beeps.]

M Hey Maria, it's Nick. I'm in town for the weekend. <u>How about hanging out</u> sometime? We can do something <u>any time Saturday</u>. Sunday afternoon is free, too, but I'm <u>leaving Sunday night</u>. Just let me know <u>when and</u>

[자동응답기 소리]

남 Maria, 나 Nick이야. 난 이번 주말에 시내에 있을 거야. 같이 시간을 보내는 게 어때? 토요일 하루 중 어느 때든 무언가를 할 수 있을 거야. 일요일 오후도 한가해. 일요일 밤에는 떠나야 해. 언제 어디서 만날 수 있는지 알려줘. 이 메시지 들으면 내게 전화하고. 고마워, 안녕.

where we should meet. Please call me back when you get this message. Thanks, bye.

Question When is the man leaving?

질문 남자는 언제 떠나나요?

4

W Jim, it's already 5:15. When do you think our second train will arrive?

여 Jim, 벌써 5시 15분이야. 두 번째 열차가 언제 도착할 것 같니?

M I have no idea. It should have arrived by now.

남 모르겠어. 지금쯤 도착했어야 하는데.

W Oh, we should have taken a bus instead of the subway.

여 아. 우린 지하철 대신 버스를 타야 했어.

M Well, the restaurant is only a few blocks away now. How about we walk the rest of the way?

남 음. 레스토랑은 여기서 몇 블록만 가면 되잖아. 나머지 길은 걸어가는 게 어때?

W I think it's going to rain.

여 비가 올 것 같아.

M I guess you're right.

남 네 말이 맞는 것 같다.

5

M Some of us are going out for pizza after work. How about joining us, Debbie?

남 우리들은 퇴근 후에 피자를 먹으러 갈 거야. Debbie 너도 같이 가는 게 어때?

W Why not? I haven't eaten all day. Where shall we meet?

여 좋아. 난 하루 종일 아무 것도 못 먹었어. 어디서 만날까?

M I know this great place called The Magic Mushroom.

남 난 Magic Mushroom이라고 불리는 멋진 곳을 알아.

W Hmm. I've never heard of it. How do you get there?

여 음. 난 들어본 적 없는데. 거기 어떻게 가니?

M Okay. Drive west on Park Street, past the mall. Turn right at the traffic light, and then turn left on the first street.

남 좋아. 쇼핑몰을 지나, Park 가에서 서쪽 방향으로 운전해. 신호등에서 우회전하고 첫 번째 거리에서 좌회전해.

W So it's on this street?

여 그럼 그 거리에 있니?

M Yeah. Second building on the right.

남 응. 오른쪽의 두 번째 건물이야.

6

M Oh, I'm so out of shape. I need to start exercising.

남 오, 내 몸매가 엉망이군. 난 운동을 시작해야겠어.

W How about joining a gym? They have all kinds of machines and exercise programs

여 헬스장에 등록하는 게 어때? 운동 기계와 프로그램들 종류가 많잖아. 우리 헬스장은 한 달에 15달러 밖에 안 내.

there. At my gym, I only pay $15 a month.

M Hmm. That's not a bad deal. Where do you go?

W Great Fitness Gym over in Huntsville.

M Well, it's too far from my house. I think I'll just start jogging.

| Vocabulary | out of shape 몸매가 엉망인, 건강이 안 좋은   machine 기계   deal 거래, 조건 |

M So, what did you think about the movie?

W I enjoyed that movie. What about you?

M Well, I liked the story, but I didn't think the acting was that good.

W Yeah, I agree.

M Hey, aren't you hungry? Why don't we go out for some dinner?

| Vocabulary | agree 동의하다 |

W I'd like to thank everyone for showing up. This meeting is about the city's new office complex. Many trees must be cut down for this new building. It will also cost millions of dollars. Why don't we spend that money on something else? We could use it to repair the old office complex instead.

| Vocabulary | show up 나타나다   office complex 사무실 단지   tear down 베다, 헐다   repair 수리하다 |

남 음. 나쁘지 않은 조건이네. 어디에 다녀?

여 Huntsville에 있는 Great Fitness Gym에 다녀.

남 음, 우리 집에서 너무 머네. 난 그냥 조깅을 시작해야겠어.

남 영화에 대해 어떻게 생각했니?

여 나는 재미있게 봤어. 넌 어떠니?

남 음, 난 이야기는 마음에 드는데 연기가 별로 좋지 않다고 생각해.

여 그래, 나도 동의해.

남 너 배 고프지 않니? 저녁 먹으러 갈래?

여 저는 모든 분들께 와 주신 데 대한 감사를 표하고 싶습니다. 이 모임은 시의 새로운 사무실 단지에 관해 의논하는 모임입니다. 많은 나무들이 이 새로운 건물을 위해 벌목되어야 합니다. 그리고 그것은 수백만 달러의 비용이 들 것입니다. 이 돈을 다른 곳에 쓰는 것이 어떨까요? 대신 우리는 낡은 사무실 단지를 보수하는 데 그 돈을 사용할 수 있습니다.

UNIT XII WHAT DOES THAT MEAN?

p.73

01 b **02** c

03 A Mary, <u>does this sentence mean</u>, "I'm sorry?"

　　B <u>I'm afraid it's wrong.</u> It means "Thank you."

　　A One more question. <u>What does "provide" mean?</u>

　　B It means "to give."

　　A <u>How do you spell it?</u>

　　B P-r-o-v-i-d-e.

Check Up Scripts

01

W Merry Christmas, honey! Here, open this card and present first.

여 메리 크리스마스에요, 여보! 여기, 이 카드와 선물을 먼저 개봉해 봐요.

M Thank you. Hey, what does this word mean?

남 고맙군요. 어, 이 단어는 무엇을 의미하는 거요?

W It means "beloved." I wanted to get you a special kind of card for a special present.

여 그건 '사랑하는 사람'을 뜻하는 거에요. 특별한 선물을 위한 특별한 종류의 카드를 드리고 싶었어요.

M Oh! You got me that gold watch I wanted. I love it!

남 오! 내가 원했던 금시계군요. 정말 마음에 드는군!

Vocabulary	present 선물　beloved 사랑하는 사람　watch 시계

02

M Excuse me, Ms. Disney. What does this word mean?

남 실례합니다. Disney 선생님. 이 단어가 무슨 뜻이죠?

W This one? It means to wish for something.

여 이것? 그건 무언가 소망한다는 것을 의미해.

M Oh, okay. I appreciate it.

남 아, 그렇군요. 감사합니다.

W You know, if you're wondering about a word, you should look it up in the dictionary. We have some over on the bookshelf by the door.

여 어떤 단어에 대해 궁금하다면 사전을 찾아 보는 것이 좋아. 문 옆의 책꽂이 위에 몇 권 있단다.

M Okay. I'll do that.

남 네, 그렇게 할게요.

Vocabulary	wish 소망하다, 바라다　appreciate 감사하다　wonder 궁금하다　look up 찾아 보다　dictionary 사전 bookshelf 책꽂이

03

A Mary, does this sentence mean "I'm sorry?"

A Mary, 이 문장이 "미안해."를 의미하니?

B I'm afraid that's wrong. It means "Thank you."

B 틀린 것 같은데. 그건 "고마워."를 의미해.

A One more question. What does "provide"

A 질문 하나 더 할게. 'provide'는 무슨 뜻이니?

mean?

B It means "to give."

A How do you spell it?

B P-r-o-v-i-d-e.

B 그건 '주다'라는 뜻이야.

A 철자는 어떻게 되니?

B P-r-o-v-i-d-e야.

Vocabulary	sentence 문장　　wrong 틀린　　provide 주다, 제공하다　　spell 철자를 쓰다

Actual Test　　1 ①　2 ②　3 ②　4 ④　5 ②　6 ⑤　7 ④　8 ③　　| p.74

1

[The telephone rings.]

W Hello, is Jeremy there?

M Hi, Samantha. This is Jeremy.

W Hey, I'm so sorry about your biking accident. How bad were you hurt?

M Well, I have a fractured leg.

W "Fractured?" What does that word mean?

M It means "broken." I have to wear a cast for the next month.

W Oh, I'm sorry.

[전화벨 소리]

여 여보세요. Jeremy 있나요?

남 안녕. Samantha. 나 Jeremy야.

여 아. 너의 자전거 사고에 대해 유감이야. 얼마나 다친 거야?

남 음. 다리가 골절되었어.

여 'Fractured?' 그건 무슨 뜻이니?

남 '부러진'이라는 뜻이야. 나는 다음 달 까지는 깁스를 하고 있어야 해.

여 안됐구나.

Vocabulary	fractured 골절된　　wear a cast 깁스를 하다

2

M Yes! This is a wonderful day!

W You mean you got it?

M That's right. I finally got my driver's license! Now all I need is a car.

W Didn't you say your parents would give you their old car?

M Yeah. All I had to do was pass my driver's test. And I did! I can't wait to start driving everywhere.

W That's so cool!

남 좋아! 정말 멋진 날인걸!

여 합격했다는 뜻이니?

남 맞아. 난 마침내 운전면허증을 땄어! 이제 내게 필요한 건 자동차 뿐이야.

여 너의 부모님께서 쓰시던 차를 주신다고 하지 않았니?

남 맞아. 난 운전면허시험만 합격하면 됐는데. 해냈지! 난 얼른 어느 곳이든 운전을 해서 가고 싶어.

여 정말 멋지구나!

Vocabulary	driver's license 운전면허증　　pass 통과하다

3

M Hey, Rachel. I'm sorry I'm late.

W Oh. Kevin. What made you so late? I was

남 Rachel. 늦어서 미안해.

여 아. Kevin. 왜 이렇게 늦었니? 난 정말 걱정했어.

really worried about you.

M Oh, it was <u>bumper to bumper</u> out there.

W <u>What do you mean by</u> "bumper to bumper"?

M It means that there is <u>so much traffic</u>.

W Oh, I see.

Vocabulary	bumper to bumper 꼬리를 문, 교통체증이 심한

남 아, 차가 꼬리를 물고 늘어서 있어서.

여 'bumper to bumper'가 무슨 뜻이니?

남 그건 교통체증이 심하다는 뜻이야.

여 아, 그렇구나.

4

M You'll never believe this.

W <u>What do you mean</u>? Do you have good news?

M The principal tells me I can study in America with <u>a full scholarship</u>. This is <u>such a great chance</u>!

W Wow! That's wonderful, dear! I'm <u>so happy</u> for you. When do you go?

M Next month. Oh, <u>this is so exciting</u>!

남 넌 이 소식을 믿지 못할 거야!

여 무슨 뜻이니? 좋은 소식이 있어?

남 교장선생님께서 내가 전액 장학금을 받고 미국에서 공부할 수 있다고 말씀하셨어! 이건 정말 대단한 기회야!

여 와! 멋지구나. 난 정말 기뻐. 언제 가는데?

남 다음 달에. 아, 정말 흥분된다!

Vocabulary	principal 교장선생님 scholarship 장학금

5

① **M** Do you know what <u>this word means</u>?

 W I have no idea.

② **M** What should I say when I want <u>to ask</u> <u>the price</u>?

 W Not at all. <u>Go ahead</u>.

③ **M** Daisy, is this sentence correct?

 W Well, I'm afraid <u>it is wrong</u>.

④ **M** Kate, <u>you've made a mistake</u> there. The spelling isn't right.

 W Oh, <u>how do you spell it</u> then?

⑤ **M** I don't understand <u>what you</u> mean.

 W Well, <u>let me put it</u> another way.

① 남 넌 이 단어가 무슨 뜻인지 아니?

 여 모르겠어.

② 남 가격을 묻고 싶을 때 뭐라고 해야 해?

 여 전혀. 어서 하도록 해.

③ 남 Daisy, 이 문장이 옳은 문장이니?

 여 음, 틀린 것 같아.

④ 남 Kate, 너 거기에서 실수를 했어. 철자가 틀렸어.

 여 아, 그럼 철자가 어떻게 되는데?

⑤ 남 난 네가 무슨 말을 하는지 모르겠어.

 여 음, 다른 방식으로 말해 볼게.

Vocabulary	price 가격 correct 옳은 make a mistake 실수를 하다

6

W Jiwon, I think <u>you've made a mistake</u>. This spelling is incorrect.

M Really? <u>How do you spell</u> "invasion?"

여 지원아, 너 실수를 한 것 같아. 이 철자가 틀렸어.

남 정말? 그럼 'invasion'을 어떻게 쓰니?

W I-n-v-a-s-i-o-n.

M Oh, thanks.

W Is that the paper for your history class?

M Yeah. It's driving me crazy! I've been working on this paper for a week, and I've still got three more pages to write.

W Oh. When do you have to turn it in?

여 I-n-v-a-s-i-o-n이야.

남 아, 고마워.

여 그건 네 역사 수업을 위한 보고서니?

남 응. 정말 미치겠어! 난 이 보고서를 일주일째 쓰고 있는데, 아직도 3페이지나 더 써야 해.

여 아, 언제 제출해야 하는데?

Vocabulary	spelling 철자 incorrect 틀린 invasion 침략 history 역사 turn in 제출하다

W OK, class, take out your new biology textbooks. Please turn to the Table of Contents. This will show you what we'll be studying this semester. The first chapter is about food and digestion, and the second is about breathing. After that, we take Test 1 and move on to Chapters 3 and 4. Chapter 3 is about the heart and 4 deals with the blood. After this we take Test 2. After Test 2 we move on to Chapter 5, which is about disease.

여 좋아요, 학생 여러분. 새 생물 교과서를 꺼내보세요. 목차를 펴세요. 이는 우리가 이번 학기에 무엇을 공부할 것인지 보여 줍니다. 1과는 음식과 소화에 관한 것이고, 2과는 호흡에 관한 것이지요. 그 후에 우린 첫 시험을 치를 것이고 3과와 4과로 넘어갈 겁니다. 3과는 심장에 관해서, 4과는 혈액에 관해 다루고 있지요. 이 후에 두 번째 시험을 치릅니다. 그리고 나서 5과인 질병에 관해 넘어갈 겁니다.

Vocabulary	take out 꺼내다 table of contents 목차 semester 학기 digestion 소화 breathing 호흡 move on to ~로 넘어가다 deal with ~을 다루다 blood 혈액 disease 질병

M Now for your traffic report. There is a major car accident on Highway 75. Three cars crashed into each other. Five people were injured in the accident, and they were taken to the hospital. The accident has blocked all traffic on the road. The road is now closed. This has slowed down traffic everywhere.

남 이제 교통 방송 안내입니다. 고속도로 75번가에서 대형 사고가 있습니다. 세 대의 차가 서로 충돌했습니다. 사고에서 5명이 부상을 입었고, 그들은 병원으로 옮겨졌습니다. 사고는 도로 위의 모든 교통을 차단시켰습니다. 도로는 현재 폐쇄된 상태입니다. 이는 모든 곳의 교통을 정체시키고 있습니다.

Vocabulary	major 심각한 highway 고속도로 crash into 충돌하다 injured 부상을 입은 block 막다, 차단하다 slow down 정체시키다

모의고사 1회

01 ④	02 ③	03 ⑤	04 ②	05 ①	06 ①	07 ④	08 ⑤	09 ②	10 ①
11 ②	12 ④	13 ③	14 ①	15 ⑤	16 ⑤	17 ②	18 ④	19 ③	20 ⑤

01

W Derrick, can you teach me math sometime?

여 Derrick, 너 언제 내게 수학을 좀 가르쳐 줄 수 있니?

M Sure. In fact, I'm free today, if that's OK. What time should we meet?

남 물론이지. 사실, 괜찮으면 난 오늘 한가한데. 몇 시에 만날래?

W I can do it anytime after 4:00. Would 4:30 work for you?

여 난 4시 이후에 시간이 되는데. 4시 30분은 괜찮아?

M Sure. I usually tutor in the library, if that's OK.

남 그럼. 괜찮다면, 난 보통 도서관에서 가르쳐.

W Yeah, that's fine. I'll see you there.

여 응. 괜찮아. 거기서 보자.

02

W Excuse me, Mr. Johnson? I have a question.

여 실례합니다. Johnson 선생님. 질문이 있어요.

M Sure. What is it?

남 그래. 뭐니?

W Will we have an essay question on our test Friday?

여 금요일 테스트에 에세이 질문이 있나요?

M Yes. You will write an essay, but you get to choose from three topics.

남 그렇단다. 에세이를 쓰게 되겠지만 세 가지 주제 중 하나에서 선택해야 하지.

W Okay. I've had trouble with earlier essay questions. That's why I wanted to be prepared for this test.

여 그렇군요. 전 지난 번 에세이 질문들이 어려워 애를 먹었어요. 그래서 이번 테스트를 위해서는 준비를 잘 하고 싶어요.

03

M Excuse me, but when will we land in Denver?

남 실례합니다만 우리가 언제 Denver에 도착하나요?

W It will be another hour, sir. We're flying over Texas right now. Would you like any snacks or water?

여 한 시간 후에요. 현재 저희 비행기는 Texas 상공을 비행하고 있습니다. 스낵이나 물을 좀 드시겠어요?

M No, thank you. I would like some new headphones, though.

남 고맙지만 괜찮아요. 그런데 새 헤드폰을 좀 받고 싶군요.

W All right. I'll bring you some in just a minute.

여 알겠습니다. 금방 가져다 드리겠습니다.

M I appreciate it.

남 고맙습니다.

04

W	Are you ready to check out, sir?
M	Yes. I'm just getting these two DVDs, please.
W	All right. Those are on sale for just 7 dollars a piece. Anything else?
M	Uh, yeah. Add this candy bar to it, too.
W	Okay. Your total will be 16 dollars.
M	Okay. I only have a 20-dollar-bill on me.

여	대여하시겠어요?
남	네. 전 이 두 DVD를 빌리고 싶어요.
여	알겠습니다. 세일 중이라 각각 7달러 밖에 하지 않아요. 다른 필요한 게 있으신가요?
남	아, 네. 이 캔디바도 추가해주세요.
여	네. 전부 합쳐 16달러입니다.
남	그렇군요. 전 20달러 지폐밖에 없어요.

05

M	Susan, I have to leave school early today.
W	Why is that?
M	I have a doctor's appointment at 2 o'clock. He has to take some X-rays, so I won't be back in.
W	All right. I still need that report for our group project by Friday, though.
M	I know. I'll come in early tomorrow and work on it. Don't worry.

남	Susan, 난 오늘 학교를 일찍 조퇴해야 할 것 같아.
여	왜?
남	2시에 병원 예약이 되어 있어. 엑스레이를 찍어야 해서 다시 돌아오지 못할 것 같아.
여	알겠어. 하지만 금요일까지 그룹 프로젝트를 위한 보고서는 필요해.
남	알고 있어. 내일 일찍 와서 할게. 걱정하지 마.

06

M	Hi, Leslie. What's up?
W	I didn't get much sleep last night. My neighbors were playing music all night. It was so loud!
M	Whoa. Did you call the police? Or did you at least complain to the neighbors?
W	No. I don't want to talk about it anymore.

남	Leslie. 무슨 일이니?
여	난 어젯밤에 잠을 많이 자지 못했어. 이웃에서 밤새 음악을 틀어놓았거든. 너무 시끄러웠어!
남	저런. 경찰을 불렀니? 아니면 적어도 이웃에게 불평을 했니?
여	아니. 난 더 이상 그것에 관해 이야기 하고 싶지 않아.

07

M	Mom? Have you seen my backpack anywhere?
W	Sorry, dear. Where did you last leave it?
M	It was up in my room last. I left it on my television. Now I can't find it.
W	Did you check by your stereo? It's a really big mess over there.
M	No. Hey, wait a second. It was on the bed all along.
W	Well, that was pretty easy.

남	엄마. 제 책가방 못 보셨어요?
여	미안하지만 못 봤어. 마지막으로 어디다 두었니?
남	마지막으로 제 방에 두었어요. 제 텔레비전 위에 두었거든요. 지금은 찾을 수가 없네요.
여	스테레오를 확인해봤니? 저 곳은 아주 엉망진창이구나.
남	아뇨. 아, 잠깐만요. 가방은 내내 침대 위에 있었네요.
여	아, 정말 찾기가 쉬웠네.

08

W Okay, I'm almost ready to go. I just need to finish packing my suitcase.

M Uh, honey, how much stuff are you bringing?

W Let's see. I'm taking a couple of books, my laptop, my games, and some magazines.

M I don't think you'll need all that. You'll be too busy enjoying the trip. You won't have time for all that other stuff.

여 좋아요. 난 출발할 준비가 거의 되었어요. 여행 가방 싸는 것을 끝내기만 하면 되요.

남 얘야. 짐을 얼마나 가지고 갈 거니?

여 어디보자… 몇 권의 책과, 노트북, 게임기, 그리고 잡지들을 가져갈 건데요.

남 난 네가 그 모든 것들이 필요하다고 생각지 않아. 여행을 즐기느라 아주 바쁠 거야. 다른 일들을 위한 시간들은 별로 나지 않을 거야.

09

① M Hey, why don't we go to an amusement park this Saturday?

W That's a good idea.

② M How often do you go see a movie?

W I'll go see a movie after the final test.

③ M Kelly, it was such a great performance!

W Thanks. It's very nice of you to say so.

④ M Will you please help me with my math homework?

W Sorry, but I'm too busy now.

⑤ M I want to get good grades.

W Then how about joining our study group?

① 남 이봐. 이번 주 토요일에 유원지에 가는 게 어때?

여 좋은 생각이야.

② 남 넌 얼마나 자주 영화를 보러 가니?

여 난 기말 고사가 끝나고 영화를 볼 거야.

③ 남 Kelly. 정말 훌륭한 공연이었어!

여 고마워. 그렇게 말해주다니 친절하구나.

④ 남 내 수학 숙제 좀 도와 줄래?

여 미안하지만 지금 너무 바빠.

⑤ 남 난 좋은 성적을 받고 싶어.

여 그럼 우리 스터디 그룹에 들어오는 게 어떠니?

10

M Hey, Margaret. I heard that your cat had some kittens.

W Yeah, she did. We have six little kittens running around our house now. We don't know what to do with them all.

M Would you mind giving me one? I've always wanted a pet.

W Yeah, that would be fine. Come by later and see which one you want.

남 Margaret. 난 너희 집 고양이가 새끼를 낳았다고 들었어.

여 응. 이제 우리에겐 집을 뛰어다니는 6마리의 아기 고양이들이 있어. 우린 아기 고양이들을 전부 어떻게 해야 할 지 모르겠어.

남 나에게 하나 주지 않을래? 난 항상 애완동물을 가지고 싶었거든.

여 그래. 그거 괜찮네. 나중에 와서 어떤 고양이가 좋을지 봐봐.

11

W May I have your attention, please? We are looking for an eight-year-old girl. Her name is Peggy Smith, and her mother said that she was missing on the third floor, near the flower shop. She has long curly hair, and is wearing a long-sleeved white shirt and blue skirt. If you see this girl, please call us at 625-1212. Thank you.

여 잠시 주목해주세요. 저희는 8살짜리 여자 아이를 찾고 있습니다. 아이의 이름은 이고 어머니께서 말씀하시길, 3층 꽃가게 근처에서 잃어버렸다고 합니다. 아이는 긴 곱슬 머리에 긴 소매의 하얀 셔츠와 파란 치마를 입고 있습니다. 이 여자아이를 보시면 625-1212로 전화주세요. 감사합니다.

12

M Maria, which do you like better, tennis or squash?

W Well, I don't like either of them.

M Oh, really? Then what is your favorite sport?

W Well, my favorite one is cycling. It's a great way to burn up many calories.

M Well, my favorite one is tennis. But I hate to do outdoor activities in the summer, so I often go swimming now.

Question What is the girl's favorite sport?

남 Maria. 넌 테니스와 스쿼시 중 어떤 것이 더 좋니?

여 음. 난 둘 다 별로야.

남 아. 정말? 그럼 네가 가장 좋아하는 운동이 뭔데?

여 음, 내가 가장 좋아하는 건 자전거타기야. 칼로리 소모가 많이 되는 좋은 방법이지.

남 음. 내가 가장 좋아하는 건 테니스야. 하지만 난 여름엔 실외활동을 하기 싫어해서. 지금은 수영을 자주 가.

질문 여자가 가장 좋아하는 운동은 무엇인가요?

13

W Jerry! I heard the great news. Congratulations!

M Thanks. My family is really excited. It's so hard to believe my sister is going to be a mom.

W I think your sister will do a fine job. So when is the baby due?

M November. That's six months away, but the time will pass quickly.

여 Jerry! 기쁜 소식을 들었어. 축하해!

남 고마워. 우리 가족은 정말 흥분해 있어. 나의 누나가 엄마가 될 거라니 믿기 힘들어.

여 난 네 누나가 정말 잘 해 낼 거라고 생각해. 언제 출산 예정이니?

남 11월이야. 6개월 남았지만 시간은 빨리 흐를 거야.

14

M Hey, Stacey. I heard that you're going on a camping trip next week.

W Yeah. The first thing I'll do there is hike up a mountain. Then I want to explore this really cool cave there.

M It sounds like fun!

남 Stacey. 난 네가 다음 주에 캠핑을 간다고 들었어.

여 응. 그 곳에서 처음으로 할 일은 등산을 하는 거야. 그런 다음 그 곳의 멋진 동굴을 탐험하고 싶어.

남 재미있겠다!

W The day after that, I will go rafting down the river.

M That sounds exciting, too. But will you do any quiet activities?

W Yeah. I will do a little fishing on the last day.

15

M Now it's time for sports news. Everyone in the city is getting ready for the national basketball championship. The Lions will play the Eagles to decide the best basketball team in the nation. The game will take place Friday night, and you can buy tickets starting on Tuesday.

16

M I don't believe this!

W What is it, Eric?

M I got good grades on my final exams, like my mom wanted. So I was certain that she'd raise my allowance this week.

W You mean she didn't?

M Yeah. I'm so disappointed!

W Oh, that's too bad. But no one knows for sure that something will happen until it actually does happen.

17

M First, you need a cup of boiling water. Most people boil the water in one of two ways. Some like to microwave it in a cup quickly. Others like to boil the water in a kettle. Either way, pour the boiling water in a teacup or pitcher. Then put one, two, or even more bags in the water. Let the bags sit for three to five minutes. Afterwards, remove the bags, drink, and enjoy!

여 그 다음날은 강가에서 래프팅을 할 거야.

남 그것도 신나겠는데. 하지만 조용한 활동은 없니?

여 있어. 난 마지막 날에 낚시를 할 거야.

남 이제 스포츠 뉴스를 전해드릴 시간입니다. 도시의 모든 사람들이 국내 농구 챔피언전을 관람할 준비가 되었습니다. 누가 국내의 최고 농구팀인지 결정하기 위해 Lions 팀과 Eagles 팀이 경기를 펼칠 예정입니다. 경기는 금요일 밤에 열릴 것이고, 화요일부터 표를 구입하실 수 있습니다.

남 믿을 수가 없어!

여 왜 그러니, Eric?

남 난 엄마가 원하신 대로 기말고사에서 좋은 성적을 받았어. 그래서 엄마가 이번 주에 내 용돈을 올려주실 거라고 확신했거든.

여 어머니께서 용돈을 안 올려주셨다는 뜻이니?

남 응. 너무 실망스러워!

여 아, 안됐구나. 하지만 어떤 일이 실제로 일어나기 전까진 아무도 그 일이 일어날 것이라고 확신할 수 없는 법이지.

남 우선, 끓인 물 한 컵이 필요합니다. 대부분의 사람들은 두 가지 중 하나의 방식으로 물을 끓입니다. 어떤 이들은 전자레인지에 컵을 빨리 데우는 것을 좋아합니다. 다른 이들은 주전자에 물을 끓이는 것을 좋아합니다. 어떤 식이든, 끓는 물을 찻잔이나 물주전자에 부으세요. 그런 다음, 하나 또는 둘, 혹은 그 이상의 티백을 물에 넣으세요. 티백이 3분에서 5분 정도 우려 나오도록 두세요. 그 다음, 티백을 제거하고, 즐겁게 마시세요!

18

W Alan! Is that you?

M Beth! Hey, how are you? It's been such a long time.

W I know. I haven't seen you since we graduated from college.

M That was five years ago! Has it been that long?

W It sure has. Say, did you ever go to law school?

M I decided not to do that. I'm actually training to become a doctor now.

W Wow, that's great! I'm actually a teacher at a middle school now.

M Cool.

여 Alan! 너니?

남 Beth! 어떻게 지내니? 정말 오랜만이다.

여 그러게. 대학 졸업 후에 널 보지 못했어.

남 5년 전이구나! 그렇게 오래되었나?

여 그래. 저, 넌 법대는 갔어?

남 난 가지 않기로 결정했어. 난 사실 지금 의사가 되기 위한 과정에 있어.

여 와. 대단하네! 난 사실 지금 중학교 교사야.

남 멋지네.

19

W Have you ever heard of the band Lovely Dream?

M I don't think so. What kind of music do they play?

W Rock and blues. They are really good!

M Oh, I didn't know that you are interested in rock. Do you have their albums?

W Yes. I'm a big fan of them.

M Could I borrow some of their stuff?

여 너 Lovely Dream이라는 밴드에 대해 들어봤니?

남 아니. 어떤 음악을 하는데?

여 록과 블루스. 정말 좋아!

남 아, 난 네가 록에 관심이 있는 줄 몰랐는데. 그들의 앨범을 가지고 있니?

여 응. 난 그들의 엄청난 팬이거든.

남 앨범을 내게 좀 빌려 줄래?

20

W Good morning, Peter. How are you feeling today?

M I feel terrible.

W Oh, why is that? Tell me what happened.

M Well, I had a big fight with Jim yesterday.

W I thought you two were best friends.

M Not anymore. I said something mean to him, and he's still mad at me. He said he won't speak to me ever again. What should I do?

여 좋은 아침이야. Peter. 오늘 기분이 어떠니?

남 최악이야.

여 오, 왜 그래? 무슨 일이 있었는지 말해봐.

남 음. 난 어제 Jim과 크게 싸웠어.

여 난 너희가 절친한 사이인 줄 알았는데.

남 더 이상은 아냐. 내가 그 애에게 못된 말을 해서 내게 아직 화가 나 있어. 그 앤 내게 다시는 말 걸지 않겠다고 했어. 어쩌면 좋지?

모의고사 2회

<table>
<tr><td>01 ②</td><td>02 ③</td><td>03 ④</td><td>04 ②</td><td>05 ⑤</td><td>06 ④</td><td>07 ①</td><td>08 ③</td><td>09 ①</td><td>10 ④</td></tr>
<tr><td>11 ⑤</td><td>12 ③</td><td>13 ④</td><td>14 ①</td><td>15 ②</td><td>16 ⑤</td><td>17 ③</td><td>18 ①</td><td>19 ①</td><td>20 ⑤</td></tr>
</table>

01

M ① She is walking a dog.

② He is lifting weights.

③ They are enjoying a meal together.

④ She is taking a picture of a tiger.

⑤ They are flying a kite.

남 ① 그녀는 강아지를 산책시키고 있다.

② 그는 역기를 들고 있다.

③ 그들은 함께 식사를 즐기고 있다.

④ 그녀는 호랑이 사진을 찍고 있다.

⑤ 그들은 연을 날리고 있다.

02

[The telephone rings.]

M Hello. Can I speak to Maggie, please?

W Sorry, but there is no one here by that name. Can I ask you what number you're trying to call?

M Isn't this 783-2019?

W No, you have the wrong number. This is 783-2009.

M Oh, I'm really sorry.

[전화벨 소리]

남 여보세요. Maggie 있나요?

여 죄송하지만 여기 그런 사람 없는데요. 몇 번으로 전화하시려 한 건가요?

남 783-2019 아닌가요?

여 아뇨. 잘못 거셨어요. 783-2009에요.

남 아. 정말 죄송합니다.

03

M Welcome to the Milkshake Castle! How can I serve you today?

W What kind of flavors do you have?

M Well, we have over 30 different flavors here. My personal favorite is peach. However, most of our customers like the Chocolate Shake.

W I do like chocolate. But I want to try something else today. I'll try the Mixed Berry, please. But please make it a small.

M Excellent choice.

남 Milkshake Castle에 오신 것을 환영합니다! 무엇을 드릴까요?

여 어떤 맛이 있나요?

남 음. 30가지도 넘는 맛이 있답니다. 제가 개인적으로 가장 좋아하는 것은 복숭아맛입니다. 하지만 손님들 대부분이 초콜릿 쉐이크를 좋아하시죠.

여 전 초콜릿을 정말 좋아하지만 오늘은 다른 것을 먹어보고 싶네요. Mixed Berry로 주세요. 작은 사이즈로요.

남 훌륭한 선택이십니다.

04

M Ms. Paulson, can I ask you a question?

W What is it, Henry?

M When will our research paper be due?

W It will be due on March 15th. That gives you an entire week to work on it.

M Okay. But what will we have to write about?

W I'll talk about that more after today's lesson.

남 Paulson 선생님. 질문을 하나 해도 되나요?

여 무엇이니. Henry?

남 언제까지 조사 보고서를 내야 하죠?

여 3월 15일까지야. 보고서를 준비할 시간이 1주일 남았지.

남 그렇군요. 하지만 어떤 것에 대해 써야 하나요?

여 오늘 수업 후에 더 이야기해주마.

05

W Good morning. How can I help you today?

M Hi. I'd like to put this money in my savings account, please. I also need some more checks.

W Yes, sir. May I see your driver's license, please?

M Sure. Oh, and can I see how much money's in my checking account?

W Yes, sir. You have $1500 in your checking account.

M Whoa! That's more than I thought.

여 좋은 아침입니다. 어떻게 도와드릴까요?

남 안녕하세요. 전 이 돈을 제 보통 예금 계좌에 넣고 싶어요. 그리고 수표도 좀 필요합니다.

여 네. 운전면허증을 보여 주시겠어요?

남 물론이죠. 아. 그리고 제 당좌 예금 계좌에 얼마나 있는지 알 수 있을까요?

여 네. 1,500달러가 있습니다.

남 우와. 제 생각보다 많군요.

06

① **M** Would you like some more chocolate cake?

   W Thanks, but I'm full.

② **M** I'm so upset! My sister lost my favorite DVD.

   W Hey, calm down.

③ **M** Please tell me if this sentence is correct.

   W I'm afraid it's wrong.

④ **M** You'd better not touch the painting.

   W I think this painting is better than that one.

⑤ **M** How about playing badminton after class?

   W Sounds good.

① **남** 초콜릿 케이크를 더 먹을래?

   여 고맙지만 배가 불러.

② **남** 난 너무 화나. 내 여동생이 내가 좋아하는 DVD를 잃어버렸어.

   여 이봐, 진정해.

③ **남** 이 문장이 맞는지 말해줘.

   여 미안하지만 틀렸어.

④ **남** 넌 그 그림을 만지지 않는 게 좋을 거야.

   여 난 이 그림이 저 것보다 낫다고 생각해.

⑤ **남** 방과 후에 배드민턴 치는 게 어때?

   여 좋아.

[The telephone rings.]

M Hello, is Ms. Beckett there?

W This is she. May I ask who's calling?

M My name is Ryan, and I'm with Richmond Cleaning Supplies. We have a special offer for you. It's our new and improved household cleaner.

W Sorry. I appreciate it, but I'm not interested. Goodbye.

[전화벨 소리]

남 여보세요. Beckett 부인 계신가요?

여 전데요. 누구신지 물어봐도 될까요?

남 제 이름은 Ryan이고, Richmond 청소 용품점의 직원입니다. 저희에겐 당신을 위한 특별한 제안이 있습니다. 우리의 신상품이자 기능이 향상된 가정용 청소기에 관해서입니다.

여 죄송합니다. 말씀은 감사하지만 관심이 없어서요. 이만 끊겠어요.

08

W Hey, Austin. I'm having a party at my house Saturday night. You want to come?

M Sure. How do I get to your house?

W Let's see. Do you know where the computer store is?

M Yeah.

W Drive north past that store. There is a neighborhood across the street. Keep driving until you get to a stop sign. Turn right at that stop sign. My house is the first one on the right.

M Great. I'll be there!

여 Austin, 난 토요일 밤에 우리 집에서 파티를 열 거야. 너도 오길 원하니?

남 물론이지. 너희 집에 어떻게 가면 되니?

여 어디 보자. 너 컴퓨터 상점이 어딘지 아니?

남 응.

여 그 상점을 지나 북쪽으로 운전해. 길 건너에 주택가가 있어. 정지 표지판을 볼 때까지 계속 운전해. 그 표지판에서 우회전해. 우리 집은 오른쪽 첫 번째 집이야.

남 좋아. 파티에 갈게!

09

W Mike, can I talk to you for a minute?

M Sure. What is it, Linda?

W I'm having a hard time making friends at my new school. What should I do?

M Hmm. I think you should try saying nice things to others. In other words, say things like, "Oh, you look really great in that pink dress," or "I really love your new haircut. Where did you get your hair done?"

W Oh, I see. Thanks for the advice.

M You're welcome. Hey, don't worry too much. I'm sure you will make new friends.

여 Mike, 잠깐 얘기 좀 할 수 있을까?

남 그럼. 무엇 때문에 그러니, Linda?

여 난 새로운 학교에서 친구를 사귀는 일에 어려움을 겪고 있어. 어떻게 해야 할까?

남 음. 난 네가 다른 사람들에게 칭찬을 해 보는 것이 좋을 것 같은데. 다시 말해서, "오, 넌 그 분홍 드레스가 정말 잘 어울리는구나."라든가, "난 네 새로운 머리 모양이 정말 마음에 들어. 어디서 머리를 했니?"라고 말해봐.

여 아, 알겠어. 충고 고마워.

남 천만에. 너무 걱정하지는 마. 난 네가 새로운 친구들을 사귈 수 있다고 확신해.

10

M Excuse me, can you help me?

W Certainly, sir. What is it that you need?

M I'm looking for cat food. Which aisle is that on?

W Aisle 12. Just walk all the way to those drinks. Then turn left, and it will be next to the dog supplies.

M Thanks.

Question What does the man want to buy?

남 실례합니다. 저를 좀 도와주시겠어요?

여 물론입니다. 무엇이 필요하신가요?

남 전 고양이 사료를 찾고 있어요. 어느 통로에 있나요?

여 12번 통로에 있어요. 저기 음료들이 있는 곳까지 쭉 걸어가세요. 그리고 왼쪽으로 도시면 강아지 용품 옆에 있을 거에요.

남 고맙습니다.

질문 남자가 사길 원하는 것은 무엇인가요?

11

W Good morning, Mr. Johnson. Please have a seat.

M Thank you. So, did you like my article?

W Yeah, overall, it was great. But we can't print it in our magazine yet.

M Why is that?

W Well, you have to correct some spelling mistakes.

M Okay. Is there anything else?

W No, that's all.

여 좋은 아침입니다. Johnson씨. 자리에 앉으세요.

남 감사합니다. 음, 제 글이 마음에 드셨다고요?

여 네, 대체적으로 훌륭했어요. 하지만 아직 잡지에 실 수 없을 것 같아요.

남 왜죠?

여 음, 몇 가지 철자 오류를 바로 잡아야 합니다.

남 알겠어요. 다른 건 없나요?

여 그게 전부입니다.

12

[The answering machine beeps.]

W Hey, Bob. It's your sister Wendy. I was wondering if you wanted to meet me for lunch tomorrow. I'd like to meet at noon, if that's OK with you. How do you feel about pizza? I know this great place downtown. I'd love to show you it. Anyway, call me back and let me know. Talk to you later. Bye.

[자동응답기 소리]

여 Bob. 누나 Wendy야. 난 네가 내일 점심에 날 만나고 싶은지 물어보고 싶구나. 네가 괜찮다면 정오에 만나고 싶은데. 피자는 어떠니? 난 시내에 아주 맛있는 곳을 알고 있어. 네게 보여주고 싶구나. 어쨌든 내게 다시 전화해서 알려줘. 나중에 얘기하자. 안녕.

13

M What are you reading Lisa?

W Hi, Chris. I'm reading poetry. It's one of my favorite poems by Sylvia Plath. Have you ever read her poetry?

M No, I've only read her novel in class.

W Well, her novel is great too, but I like her poetry more.

남 무엇을 읽고 있니, Lisa?

여 안녕. Chris. 난 시를 읽고 있어. Sylvia Plath가 쓴 내가 가장 좋아하는 시 중 하나야. 넌 그녀의 시를 읽어본 적 있니?

남 아니. 난 수업 시간에 소설만 읽어 봤어.

여 음, 소설도 좋지만, 난 그녀의 시가 더 좋아.

M It looks like you're really into poetry, huh?	**남** 넌 정말 시를 아주 좋아하는 것 같구나.
W Yeah, I really am. I love reading poetry in my spare time.	**여** 응. 정말 좋아해. 난 여가 시간에 시를 읽는 게 너무 좋아.
M Have you ever thought about writing poetry yourself?	**남** 직접 시를 써 볼 생각을 해 본 적 있니?
W No. I'm not a very good writer.	**여** 아니. 난 글을 잘 못 써.

14

M Hey, Carol, have you seen *"The Jackpot"* yet?	**남** Carol. 너 「The Jackpot」을 아직 안 봤니?
W No, I haven't. Why? Have you seen it?	**여** 아니. 왜? 넌 봤니?
M Yeah. I went to see it with some friends last weekend. It was really great!	**남** 응. 난 지난 주말에 친구들과 보러 갔어. 정말 재미있었어!
W That's interesting. Is there a lot of action in it?	**여** 흥미롭구나. 액션이 많니?
M Not really. It's basically a comedy.	**남** 별로. 그건 기본적으로 코미디야.
W Hmm. I might check it out sometime.	**여** 음. 언제 한 번 보러 가야겠구나.

15

W Hey, Harold. What's going on?	**여** Harold. 어떻게 지내?
M Not much. I just took my last final exam.	**남** 별로 특별한 건 없어. 난 방금 마지막 기말 고사를 봤어.
W Wow. You must be exhausted.	**여** 와. 피곤하겠네.
M Eh, not really. I'm glad it's over, but I'm not tired at all.	**남** 아. 별로. 난 시험이 끝나서 기쁘지만 전혀 피곤하지 않아.
W Was it really hard?	**여** 많이 어려웠니?
M Nah. I'm sure I did great on it. So I'm going to take it easy for the rest of the day.	**남** 아니. 난 잘 쳤다고 확신해. 그래서 남은 시간을 아주 편안한 마음으로 보낼 거야.
W Sounds like a good idea.	**여** 좋은 생각 같구나.

16

M It's taking forever to get to work! Why aren't we moving faster?	**남** 출근하는 데 시간이 너무 걸리잖아! 왜 좀 더 빨리 움직이지 않는 거지?
W It's rush hour. That's why there are so many passengers. But it's much more crowded up on the roads.	**여** 출퇴근 시간이잖아. 그래서 승객들도 많은 거고. 하지만 길 위에는 훨씬 더 붐빌 거야.
M Yeah, I know. That's why I don't drive to work. I just wish we'd hurry up.	**남** 그래, 알아. 그래서 내가 자동차로 출근하지 않는 거지. 난 그저 우리가 서둘러 갔으면 좋겠어.
W Just be patient. We only have a few more stops.	**여** 참아. 우린 몇 번의 역만 더 지나면 돼.

17

W Jason, you are shaking your leg again!

M Oh, Mom. I didn't notice that I was shaking my leg.

W I think I told you not to do that, like a million times. It makes others feel uncomfortable.

M Sorry, Mom. You know it's really hard to break a bad habit.

W I know. But just try to be more careful.

M Okay, Mom.

여 Jason, 너 또 다리를 떨고 있구나!

남 아, 엄마. 난 다리를 떨고 있는지 알아채지 못했어요.

여 그러지 말라고 수 백 번이나 얘기했던 것 같은데. 그러면 남들이 불편함을 느낀다고.

남 죄송해요, 엄마. 나쁜 습관을 고치는 게 정말 힘들다는 거 아시잖아요.

여 알지. 하지만 좀 더 주의하도록 해.

남 알았어요, 엄마.

18

M I can't believe this. My mom wants me to find a part-time job over the summer!

W Well, what's wrong with that?

M But I just turned 16, and I wanted to enjoy my summer break. Now I won't have any freedom.

W Well, that might be true. But I think you should follow your mother's advice. Taking a part-time job will be good experience for future jobs.

남 믿을 수가 없어. 우리 엄마는 내가 여름 동안 아르바이트를 하길 원하셔.

여 음. 그게 뭐가 잘못된 건데?

남 하지만 난 이제 16살이 되었고 여름 방학을 즐기고 싶었어. 이제 자유가 없을 거 아냐.

여 음. 그건 사실일지도 몰라. 하지만 난 네 어머니 충고를 따라야 한다고 생각해. 아르바이트는 미래의 직업을 위한 좋은 경험이 될 거야.

19

M Wow, that's a nice coat, Alicia.

W Thank you, Jim. It was a present from my mom. It's the nicest coat I have.

M Do you know where she got it? My dad and I would love to get my mom something like that for her birthday.

W She got it from J.J. Richmond's in Cedar City. I heard that they're having a sale now.

M Do you know how long the store will have this sale?

남 와, 멋진 코트구나, Alicia.

여 고마워, Jim. 이건 우리 엄마께서 내게 주신 선물이었어. 내가 가진 코트 중 제일 근사하지.

남 어디서 사셨는지 아니? 우리 아빠와 난 엄마 생신에 그것과 같은 선물을 해주고 싶은데.

여 Cedar City에 있는 JJ. Richmond's에서 사셨어. 난 그 곳에서 요즘 세일을 하고 있다고 들었는데.

남 세일 기간이 얼마동안인지 아니?

20

W Tomorrow is my birthday, and my parents said I could have one big present. I have to decide between two things. One is a new computer, and the other is a summer trip to England. I'd like to have both. However, the computer I have right now still works fine. But this might be my only chance to ever go to England. And there's so much I'd like to see there. That's why…

여 내일은 내 생일이고, 우리 부모님께서는 내게 엄청난 선물이 있다고 말씀하셨다. 난 두 가지 중 하나를 선택해야 한다. 하나는 새 컴퓨터이고, 다른 하나는 영국으로의 여름 여행이다. 난 둘 다 가지고 싶다. 하지만 지금 내가 가지고 있는 컴퓨터는 아직 잘 작동한다. 하지만 이것은 영국으로 갈 수 있는 유일한 기회일지도 모른다. 그리고 그 곳에서 보고 싶은 것들도 너무 많다. 그래서…

모의고사 3회

01 ①	**02** ④	**03** ①	**04** ③	**05** ④	**06** ③	**07** ②	**08** ③	**09** ⑤	**10** ①
11 ②	**12** ③	**13** ⑤	**14** ②	**15** ⑤	**16** ①	**17** ④	**18** ②	**19** ③	**20** ④

01

W Did you know Carla's birthday is coming up?	**여** 너 Carla의 생일이 다가오고 있는 거 알았니?
M Yeah, I know.	**남** 응. 알아.
W So, did you get her a birthday present yet?	**여** 그럼 생일 선물은 샀니?
M Well, not yet. I just have no idea what to get her.	**남** 아니. 아직. 난 뭘 사야 할 지 모르겠어.
W Hmm. Well, she is a big fan of classical music. Maybe you should buy her a classical music record.	**여** 음. 그 앤 클래식 음악을 아주 좋아해. 클래식 음반을 사 주면 좋을 것 같은데.
M Well, I don't want to give her a record she already has.	**남** 음. 난 그 애가 이미 가지고 있는 음반을 주고 싶지 않은데.
W Then how about a picture frame? She really likes to take pictures.	**여** 그럼 사진 액자를 사주는 건 어때? 사진찍는 것을 정말 좋아하니까.
M That's a good idea. Thanks.	**남** 좋은 생각이구나. 고마워.

02

[The telephone rings.]	[전화벨 소리]
W Hello. This is the Lennox Museum. How can I help you?	**여** 여보세요. Lennox 박물관입니다. 어떻게 도와드릴까요?
M Hi, I was calling to set up a tour next Thursday. It's for my students.	**남** 안녕하세요, 전 다음 주 목요일 방문을 준비하기 위해 전화 드렸습니다. 제 학생들을 위한 것이죠.
W Okay, sir. How many people will be in your group?	**여** 알겠습니다. 인원은 몇 명인가요?
M Twenty-seven total. Also, I'd like to begin at the earliest time. When would that be?	**남** 전부 합쳐 27명입니다. 그리고 가장 이른 시간에 시작하고 싶은데요. 그게 언제가 될까요?
W Our first tour begins at 9:30 a.m., sir.	**여** 저희의 첫 투어는 오전 9시 30분에 시작합니다.

03

M Last weekend I visited a farm. I'd never been before, so it was a very interesting experience. I didn't know there would be so	**남** 지난 주말, 난 농장을 방문했다. 난 전에 농장을 방문해 본 적이 한 번도 없었는데, 그것은 아주 흥미로운 경험이었다. 난 그렇게 많은 동물들이 있을지 알지 못했다! 젖소만 백

many animals! There were over a hundred cows alone. I also saw about a dozen horses. I even got to feed some chickens. I really wanted to see the pigs, but we couldn't that day. Anyway, my favorite animals there were the goats. I even got to pet one!

마리가 넘게 있었다. 그리고 여러 마리의 말들도 보았다. 난 닭들에게 모이를 주기도 했다. 난 돼지를 정말 보고 싶었는데, 그날은 볼 수 없었다. 어쨌든, 그 곳에서 내가 가장 마음에 들었던 동물은 염소였다. 난 심지어 애완용으로 한 마리를 얻기까지 했다!

04

M Can I help you?

W Yes, I'd like to exchange this dress.

M Oh, don't you like the design?

W It's not that. It's really cute. But it makes me look a little fat, I think. It's because of the color. Do you have it in black?

M Sure. Come with me.

남 도와드릴까요?

여 네, 전 이 드레스를 교환하고 싶어요.

남 아, 디자인이 마음에 안 드시나요?

여 아뇨. 정말 귀여워요. 그런데 좀 뚱뚱해 보이는 것 같아서요. 색깔 때문에요. 검정색으로 있나요?

남 물론이죠. 이쪽으로 오세요.

05

M Now for this week's weather. We will probably get a little rain today, but it will be nice and sunny tomorrow. On Thursday, there will be a strong chance of thunderstorms. Plus, we are expecting pretty bad weather during this weekend. It's just windy and cloudy on Friday, but there will be lots of rain on Saturday and Sunday. Temperatures will be a lot cooler, too.

남 금주의 날씨입니다. 오늘은 아마 비가 약간 오겠지만 내일은 맑고 화창할 것입니다. 목요일에는 폭풍우가 있을 가능성이 높습니다. 그리고, 이번 주말 동안 악천후가 예상됩니다. 금요일에는 바람이 불고 흐리다가 토요일과 일요일에는 비가 많이 올 것입니다. 기온도 훨씬 떨어질 것입니다.

06

W Ladies and gentlemen, I am happy to speak to you tonight. I have served this city for over ten years. With your help, I'd like to serve longer. We can make this a safer place for our families. We can bring in more jobs, better jobs. Just vote for me in the upcoming election. I won't let you down!

여 신사 숙녀 여러분, 오늘 밤 여러분께 이 말씀을 드릴 수 있어 기쁩니다. 저는 10년 이상이나 이 도시를 위해 일했습니다. 여러분의 도움으로 저는 더 오래 일하고 싶습니다. 우리는 이 도시를 우리 가족을 위해 더 안전한 곳이 되도록 만들 수 있습니다. 우린 또한 더 많고 더 좋은 일자리를 창출할 수 있습니다. 다가오는 선거일에 제게 투표하십시오. 실망시켜 드리지 않을 것입니다!

07

M Hi, dear. How was school?

W It was OK, dad. I had a big test today, but I think I did OK.

M That's good to hear. Your mom is making dinner at home.

W Great. Hey, can we stop by the library real

남 안녕, 딸아. 학교는 어땠니?

여 괜찮았어요, 아빠. 오늘 중요한 시험이 있었는데 잘 친 것 같아요.

남 그렇다니 기쁘구나. 엄마가 집에서 저녁을 하고 계신단다.

여 좋군요. 아, 도서관에 잠깐만 들렀다 갈 수 있을까요? 책

quickly? I have to return some books.

M Yeah, we can do that.

W Thanks.

08

M Excuse me. Do you sell any plastic containers here?

W Yes, sir. How many do you need?

M Hmm. I'm not sure. They're for a party next Thursday. I'm fixing a special fruit punch for a lot of people.

W How much are you fixing?

M I'm going to prepare about 35 liters of it. I think I'll need three of the 10-liter containers and a 5-liter container.

W Okay. Here you are.

남 실례합니다. 이 곳에서 플라스틱 용기를 파나요?

여 네. 몇 개나 필요하세요?

남 음. 확실치 않은데요. 다음 주 목요일 파티를 위한 겁니다. 전 많은 사람들을 위해 특별한 과일 펀치를 담그려고 하거든요.

여 얼마나 많이 담그세요?

남 35리터 정도 준비하려고 합니다. 10리터 용기 세 개와 5리터 용기 하나면 되겠군요.

여 네. 여기 있습니다.

09

W Hey, Bill. I heard that you have an old Corvette.

M Yeah. I don't drive it anymore, though. It needs a few repairs.

W Would you be interested in selling it? My husband is good with cars. He could fix it up for me, and you could make a little money.

M That's not a bad idea. But I'll have to check with my wife first.

여 Bill, 난 네가 낡은 Corvette자동차를 가지고 있다고 들었어.

남 응. 하지만 난 그것을 더 이상 운전하지 않아. 수리가 좀 필요해.

여 혹시 그 차를 파는 데 관심 있니? 우리 남편이 차를 잘 다루는데. 남편이 나를 위해 그 차를 수리하고, 넌 돈을 좀 벌 수도 있을 거야.

남 괜찮은 생각이네. 하지만 아내에게 먼저 물어봐야 해.

10

W I heard that your team's in the baseball championship tomorrow, Ronald.

M Yeah! We won the most games this season. We just have to win one more. Then we'll be the best team in the league!

W That's a pretty big game.

M Yeah, but I can hardly wait! I want to get out there so badly. I'm going to play my best out there and win!

여 너희 팀이 내일 야구 챔피언전에 출전한다고 들었어, Ronald.

남 응! 우린 이번 시즌 대부분의 경기에서 승리했어. 한번만 더 이기면 되는 거지. 그러면 우리는 리그에서 최고의 팀이 될 거야!

여 정말 중요한 경기구나.

남 응. 정말 기대돼! 난 정말 그 곳에 가고 싶어. 그 곳에서 최선을 다해서 이길 거야!

11

M Jessica, do you remember that we're

남 Jessica, 오늘 밤 우리가 영화 보러 가기로 한 거 기억

going to go see a movie tonight?

W Oh, I remember. When does the movie start?

M At 8 o'clock sharp. I think we should meet an hour and a half before it starts so that we can have dinner.

W Okay. Where should we meet?

M How about Joe's Cafeteria?

W Sounds good. See you then.

여 아. 기억해. 영화가 언제 시작하니?

남 8시 정각에. 난 우리가 영화 시작 한 시간 반 전에 만나야 저녁을 먹을 수 있을 것 같은데.

여 알았어. 어디서 만날까?

남 Joe's Cafeteria는 어떠니?

여 좋아. 그때 보자.

12

W Excuse me, but I'm having trouble with this diving position. Would you please help me?

M No problem. Okay, remember to keep your legs straight. This is one of the most important things.

W Keep them straight. Got it.

M After jumping, fold yourself in the middle. Then you wrap your arms around the back of your knees. Your feet should be above your head.

W Okay. I think I got it now. Thank you.

여 실례합니다. 전 이 다이빙 자세를 하는 데 어려움이 있어요. 도와 주시겠어요?

남 물론이죠. 그럼. 다리를 쭉 뻗어야 한다는 것을 기억하세요. 이것이 가장 중요한 것 중 하나입니다.

여 쭉 뻗고 있어라. 알겠어요.

남 점프를 한 뒤에. 중간에서 몸을 접으세요. 그리고 무릎 뒤로 팔을 감으세요. 발은 머리 위에 있어야 합니다.

여 알겠어요. 전 이해한 것 같아요. 감사합니다.

13

M Attention please. I'd like to remind you all of the School Picnic on Friday, April 15. The picnic will begin at noon, and there will be many fun games and sports to play! All classes must attend, and the students in each class must prepare a dish. Please decide on these dishes by this Wednesday.

남 집중하세요. 4월 15일 금요일에 있을 학교 소풍에 대해 상기시켜 드리고 싶습니다. 소풍은 정오에 시작할 예정이고 재미있는 게임과 운동을 많이 할 것입니다! 모든 학급의 학생들은 참석해야만 하고, 각 학급의 학생들은 음식을 준비해야 합니다. 이번 주 수요일까지 음식을 결정해 주세요.

14

W All right. All of these boxes are packed. We can put them in the truck now.

M Okay, but first I need to get some of this furniture.

W Do you need help with any of it?

M I'll need help lifting this couch. I can get the rest by myself.

W Okay.

여 됐어. 이 박스들 모두 다 쌌어. 우린 이제 트럭에 실으면 돼.

남 그래. 하지만 먼저 이 가구를 좀 옮겨야겠어.

여 도움이 필요하니?

남 이 소파를 들어 올리는 데 도움이 필요할 것 같아. 나머지는 혼자 할 수 있어.

여 알았어.

15

W This is not good!

M What's the matter, dear? Are you looking for the car key?

W It's the bill for our car. I can't find it anywhere.

M Hey, take it easy. I'm sure it's somewhere around here.

W But what if we don't find it?

M I can visit the office and pay them there. I'll go there after I pick up the kids from school.

여 이러면 안 되는데.

남 무슨 일이에요. 여보? 자동차 열쇠를 찾고 있는 거에요?

여 자동차 고지서요. 어디서도 찾을 수가 없어요.

남 진정해요. 여기 어딘가 있음이 틀림없어요.

여 하지만 못 찾으면 어떡하죠?

남 사무실에 들러서 그 곳에서 지불하면 되요. 학교에서 아이들을 태운 뒤 갈게요.

16

① **W** Excuse me. Could you please help me change this flat tire?

　M Sure. Let me give you a hand.

② **W** Sorry, I didn't know that I can't park here.

　M That's OK. But please be more careful next time.

③ **W** I don't think I was speeding, sir.

　M Please show me your driver's license.

④ **W** Excuse me. How can I get to the gas station?

　M Drive up the road and it'll be on your left.

⑤ **W** The traffic is really terrible today.

　M Yeah. I think there might be a car accident on the highway.

① **여** 실례합니다. 이 펑크 난 타이어 가는 것을 좀 도와주실래요?

　남 물론이죠. 도와드릴게요.

② **여** 미안합니다. 이 곳에 주차할 수 없는지 몰랐어요.

　남 괜찮아요. 다음 번엔 더 주의해 주세요.

③ **여** 제가 속도 위반을 한 것 같지 않은데요, 경관님.

　남 운전면허증을 보여주시죠.

④ **여** 실례합니다. 주유소에 어떻게 가죠?

　남 길을 쭉 따라 가면 왼쪽에 있을 겁니다.

⑤ **여** 오늘 교통정체가 정말 심하구나.

　남 응. 고속도로에서 사고가 났나 봐.

17

M Hey, Emily, when do you have your English class?

W I have it during fourth period. Why do you ask?

M I was wondering if I could borrow your notes. I have an English quiz this morning. I can give you the notes back at lunch.

W Oh, that won't work. I have lunch after my

남 Emily. 너 언제 영어 수업이 있니?

여 4교시에 있어. 왜 묻니?

남 내가 너의 노트를 좀 빌릴 수 있을까 해서. 오늘 아침에 영어 퀴즈가 있거든. 점심 시간에 노트를 다시 돌려줄게.

여 아, 안되겠는데. 난 5교시 생물학 수업 후에 점심을 먹

fifth-period biology class. I need the notes before then. Sorry.

M That's okay. I can probably borrow them from someone else.

Question When does Emily have her biology class?

어. 그 전에 노트가 필요하거든. 미안해.

남 괜찮아. 다른 사람한테 빌릴 수 있을 거야.

질문 Emily의 생물학 수업은 언제인가요?

18

M Look at that child. He's running around and yelling so loudly. It's unbelievable!

W Well, he's just a little kid. It's natural.

M I don't think so. It may not seem serious when they are little kids. But when they're older, you can't control them!

W I'm not sure about that.

M Parents need to be tougher and stricter.

남 저 아이를 봐. 뛰어다니면서 시끄럽게 소리 지르고 있어. 믿을 수가 없군!

여 음, 걘 아직 어린애잖아. 당연한 일이지.

남 난 그렇게 생각 안 해. 어린애일 때는 심각해 보이지 않을지도 모르지. 하지만 나이가 더 들면 통제를 할 수가 없게 된다고!

여 난 확실히 잘 모르겠어.

남 부모는 더 냉정하고 엄해야 한다고.

19

M Your best friend Timmy looks so worried today. So you ask him if anything's wrong. He says that he lost his brother's soccer ball a few days ago. Last night, Timmy's brother asked him if he knew where it was. He was so embarrassed and lied that he didn't know. Timmy feels really bad about the lie. In this situation, what would you say to him?

남 당신의 친한 친구 Timmy가 오늘 아주 걱정스러워 보입니다. 그래서 당신은 그에게 뭐가 잘못되었냐고 묻습니다. 그는 그가 며칠 전에 형의 축구공을 잃어버렸다고 합니다. 어젯밤, 형이 Timmy에게 축구공이 어디 있는지 아냐고 물었습니다. 그는 매우 당황해서 모른다고 거짓말을 했습니다. Timmy는 거짓말을 한 것에 대해 아주 걱정하고 있습니다. 이런 상황에서, 그에게 뭐라고 말하겠습니까?

20

W What did you do last weekend Robert?

M Well, I went to an amusement park with my family on Saturday.

W Oh, sounds like you had a good time.

M Yeah, and I went to visit Melissa at the hospital on Sunday.

W Oh, how's she doing?

M She's doing great. So is her baby.

여 지난 주말에 무엇을 했니, Robert?

남 음, 난 토요일에 가족과 유원지에 갔어.

여 아, 즐거운 시간을 보낸 것 같구나.

남 응, 그리고 일요일에는 병원에 있는 Melissa를 방문하러 갔지.

여 아, 그녀는 어떠니?

남 그녀는 건강해. 그녀의 아기도 그렇고.

센치한 Listening 길들이기

중학 영어 내신 만점을 향한 길들이기 시리즈

- 센치한 Listening 길들이기 총 6권
- 도도한 Reading 길들이기 총 6권
- 까칠한 Grammar 길들이기 총 6권

www.compasspub.com/LG